HOW TO BE A
DIFFICULT BITCH

HOW TO BE A
DIFFICULT BITCH

CLAIM YOUR POWER, DITCH THE HATERS, AND FEEL GOOD DOING IT

HALLEY BONDY
MARY C. FERNANDEZ
SHARON LYNN PRUITT-YOUNG
ZARA HANAWALT
T.L. LUKE

ZEST BOOKS
MINNEAPOLIS

To Robin and Sofia —Halley

For Niall and Serena —Zara

To my mom, who has never allowed me to stop believing.
—Mary

To my sister, my forever hypewoman. And to all the weird
Black girls: you got this. —Sharon

To my mum, who wanted to be an artist and was told to be
a secretary; thank you for encouraging me when the world
discouraged you. —T.L.L.

Zest Books™
An imprint of Lerner Publishing Group, Inc.
241 First Avenue North
Minneapolis, MN 55401 USA

For reading levels and more information, look up this title at www.lernerbooks.com.
Visit us at zestbooks.net. f

Cover and interior illustrations by T.L. Luke
Design elements: Cristina Romero Palma/Shutterstock.com; designofunique/
Shutterstock.com; Natykach Nataliia/Shutterstock.com; Philll/Shutterstock.com.

Designed by Kim Morales
Main body text set in Univers LT Std.
Typeface provided by Adobe Systems.

Library of Congress Cataloging-in-Publication Data

Names: Bondy, Halley, 1984– author.
Title: How to be a difficult bitch : claim your power, ditch the haters, and feel good doing it / Halley Bondy.
Description: Minneapolis : Zest Books, [2021] | Summary: "Being a powerhouse is a choice, a lifestyle, a code of ethics. It takes work, a thick skin, and perseverance. Learn the basics of being a Difficult Bitch, from school to friends to body to life"— Provided by publisher.
Identifiers: LCCN 2020013448 (print) | LCCN 2020013449 (ebook) | ISBN 9781541586741 (library binding) | ISBN 9781541586758 (paperback) | ISBN 9781728419138 (ebook)
Subjects: LCSH: Young women—Psychology—Juvenile literature. | Youth—Psychology—Juvenile literature. | Self-confidence—Juvenile literature. | Self-esteem—Juvenile literature. | Conduct of life—Juvenile literature.
Classification: LCC HQ1229 .B56 2021 (print) | LCC HQ1229 (ebook) | DDC 305.242/2—dc23

LC record available at https://lccn.loc.gov/2020013448
LC ebook record available at https://lccn.loc.gov/2020013449

Manufactured in the United States of America
1-47427-48006-10/15/2021

CONTENTS

LIVING WELL IS THE BEST REVENGE.

—George Herbert, 1640

INTRO
AND COMMANDMENTS

So you want to be a Difficult Bitch.

Welcome!

You'll be joining a long line of Difficult Bitches—maybe even from your own family.

(Don't worry, it's a compliment.)

Maybe your grandma was an amazing chess player. Maybe your aunt ran for city council against a bunch of old dudes. Maybe your mom or stepmom raised you to follow your dreams. Maybe your dad was the only one to stand up for LGBTQ rights in a very conservative area.

None of them would have gotten there without being a Difficult Bitch, or without being mentored by Difficult Bitches.

In some form or another, pioneering aviator Amelia Earhart was called a Difficult Bitch. Same for Grace Hopper, who invented the first computer programming language compiler. Let's not even get started on suffragists or civil rights activists, who were called all kinds of things, among them most certainly: Difficult Bitch.

If you ask me, being a Difficult Bitch is a *good* thing.

Difficult Bitches are agents of change. They're heroes who don't wear capes (or maybe they do, and that cape is *fierce*). They annoy people. They threaten the status quo. All of this is, of course, in the name of self-love, confidence, and the greater good.

You can't be a Difficult Bitch *all* the time—not without running yourself ragged. Sometimes you need a break. Sometimes being a Difficult Bitch is unsafe, or it's not considered okay in your culture.

But somewhere, there's a Difficult Bitch inside of you. You can choose when to unleash this inner self—but rest assured, the world needs her, him, or them.

Let's first address an elephant in the room here. *Bitch* is a word that has been used with many different intentions. Let's go through them.

Bitch has been used to

A. **Put down women.**
   For example, saying, "That girl is a bitch" in a mean way, when referring to a strong woman who is speaking her mind.

B. **Insult a man's masculinity.**
   For example, saying, "You are such a little bitch!" in a bullying, derogatory way in order to make a man feel like "less of a man."

C. **Playfully talk to your friends.**
   This one is all about tone and the level of friendship. You might say, "You're such a bitch!" to a friend, and if they're in on the joke, it's totally fine—everyone is laughing. But you could say the same thing to a friend and hurt their feelings. Tread lightly, and make sure that you're close with someone before you try this.

D. **#BossBitch, #HeadBitchInCharge, etc.**
   These terms and hashtags have been used to talk about people who take control. They're the ones who run companies and own their lives.

I think that we're all over A and B, right? Like, let's move on, people. Done. Delete.

C is fine as long as everyone's having fun. Whatever.

In this book, we'll be using the phrase in a way that's closest to D, but we're going to take it a step further.

Get ready, because from here on out, *Bitch* means "powerhouse."

Being a powerhouse is a choice. It's a lifestyle. It's a code of ethics. It takes work, a thick skin, and perseverance. So swig that smoothie, chant, sing, jump—do whatever it takes to get yourself pumped. In this book, you'll learn the ins and outs of being a Difficult Bitch, from school to friends to body to life.

First, some quick ground rules:

- **We'll be using she/her pronouns a lot throughout this book, but sometimes we'll use he/him or they/them, because people of any gender identity can be a Difficult Bitch and take the advice in this book. Powerhouses can be any gender or no gender. This book is for all your siblings and friends.**
- **Being a Difficult Bitch is not about being a dick or being disruptive just for the sake of getting under other people's skin. That's for a book called *How to Be F***ing Awful*. There are many people in the world who think they're Difficult Bitches but who are really just insecure and spouting nonsense.**
- **It's not about shirking responsibility and cruising through life like nothing matters. That's not being a Difficult Bitch. That's being lazy.**

Look, nobody is perfect, and if you can't follow everything in this book to a T, don't stress. Nobody can check all the boxes all the time. Just read it, let it open you up a bit, allow it to simmer, and take what you need from it. That's what a Difficult Bitch would do.

Full disclosure, readers: I'm a cis white lady. Being a

Difficult Bitch means different things to people with different backgrounds and identities from mine, so I can't write this book by myself. Some awesome, diverse women will be joining me. Being a Difficult Bitch is a community effort. I'm so honored that these women are contributing their voices.

Let's get started.

Hi! My name is SHARON PRUITT-YOUNG. I'm here throughout this book for all the Black girls, boys, and nonbinary folks out there. In a world of hypervisiblity and respectability politics, you might not feel like you can be a Difficult Bitch in the same way as other folks—so let's work through it together. If I can do it, so can you.

Hi! I'M MARY FERNANDEZ, Colombian immigrant, activist, fashion addict, and soon-to-be first blind woman MBA graduate from Duke University's business school. As a Latinx and disabled woman, I can say that my people are fabulous, bold, courageous, and beautiful. And we are here to stay!

Hi! My name is ZARA HANAWALT. I'm the only child of two immigrants from India and am passionate about breaking down stereotypes. I believe in embracing diversity in all its forms and love that this book is giving minority women some much-needed representation.

THE COMMANDMENTS

DIFFICULT BITCHES SHALL

STAND UP FOR THEMSELVES

LOVE THEMSELVES

BE THEMSELVES

HELP THOSE IN NEED

ASK FOR HELP WHEN THEY NEED IT

BE EMPATHETIC

BREAK BOUNDARIES FOR A BETTER WORLD

STAND UP FOR WHAT THEY BELIEVE IN

STAND UP FOR OTHERS

EXPERIMENT

EMBRACE DIVERSITY

BE LOUD AND PROUD

BE IMPERFECT

DO THEIR BEST

RESPECT THEMSELVES AND OTHERS

PRACTICE SAFE AND HEALTHY HABITS

LEARN FROM MISTAKES

OWN UP

DIFFICULT BITCHES SHALL NOT

BE SILENCED

BE CRUEL

BE PETTY

BE DICKS

BACK DOWN

BE APATHETIC

WORRY ABOUT HATERS

ENGAGE IN BULLSHIT

TOLERATE TOXIC BEHAVIOR

BE EXCLUSIONARY TOWARD OTHERS BECAUSE OF RACE, GENDER, SEXUALITY, DISABILITY, OR OTHERWISE

LET FEAR GET IN THE WAY

ACKNOWLEDGING YOUR OWN POWER

Empowerment is everybody's favorite buzzword these days, but it's a really, really good one for a Difficult Bitch to keep in her back pocket. According to the Oxford Dictionary, *empowerment* is "the process of becoming stronger and more confident, especially in controlling one's life and claiming one's rights." There's nothing more fundamental to being a Difficult Bitch than this.

Becoming a Difficult Empowered Bitch is a lifelong journey. It takes a lot of strength, support, and encouragement to feel empowered. When you're a little kid, everybody makes decisions for you. Slowly, as you grow up, you become more and more empowered to do your own thing. You decide when you go to bed. You decide what you're going to have for breakfast and cook it yourself. You pick your outfits.

But feeling empowered is about more than these logistics. It's about embracing your personal Difficult Bitch on the inside and letting her shine on the outside.

A Difficult Empowered Bitch doesn't rely on other people to tell her who she is. She stands up for herself and for others. She feels confident a lot of the time but can admit when she doesn't feel confident, or when she feels sad or angry—because she's not afraid of her feelings. A Difficult Empowered Bitch also knows she will never be perfect, and that's okay.

Here's how to strive to be a Difficult Empowered Bitch:

TRUST YOUR INSTINCTS

When you trust your instincts, you follow the voice inside of you instead of worrying about other influences.

Trusting your instincts is hard to do. We usually make about a million mistakes before we say something like "I should have trusted my instincts."

If a person is giving you a bad vibe, you don't need to come up with some lengthy justification for why you don't want to hang out with them. A bad vibe is a bad vibe, and you should trust your instincts and walk away. If you turn out to be wrong, what's the harm? If you're right, you dodged a bullet.

If you don't want to see a movie because you find the trailers offensive, don't. Trust your instincts no matter what anyone else has to say about the movie.

If you're not feeling soccer this season and you're feeling musical theater instead, trust your instincts and go for musical theater. Even if everyone in your life is all about sports, you're the one who gets to make decisions about your life, not them. Nobody knows your instincts like you do, and the *last* thing you want to do is kick yourself midway through the soccer season and say, "I should have trusted my instincts." (Maybe sleep on it, though. This is a pretty big decision that will affect your semester.)

That said, sometimes our instincts actually hold us back. If your instincts are coming from a place of fear or anxiety, you might miss a wonderful opportunity. Ideally, a Difficult Empowered Bitch trusts her instincts 90 percent of the time, and for the other 10 percent, she goes against her instincts to try something a little weird and different. That's the only way to grow.

So, once in a while, if your instincts are telling you NOT to go on a camping trip with your tennis team or NOT to try a regional cuisine for the first time, go for it anyway. (You know, as long as it's safe.)

REALIZE YOUR POWER

A Difficult Empowered Bitch is powerful. It doesn't matter if she's popular or perfect. A Difficult Empowered Bitch is powerful no matter what—and she *knows* it.

You have the power to make change in your school and in your society. You have the power to help people, and to make them feel good. You have the power to create things. You have the power to *feel* powerful, even if others want to marginalize you or act like they're more important than you. Sometimes it takes a bit of encouragement and experience to realize your power, but trust me, it's already inside of you.

Keep in mind, though: This doesn't mean you should go around being mean or disrespectful to friends or teachers. Realizing your power means that you *don't* act high and mighty, because you know you have the power to hurt someone's feelings and cause harm. Realize your power, own it, and then only use it for good.

HYPOTHETICAL

Consider the following story:

Violet and Jack were assigned to do a group presentation together in their world history class. Violet dreaded it. Jack was so much better than her at history. He was one of those kids who seemed to know about every subject before it was even taught. Violet thought he would make her feel stupid.

When it came time to do the project, she kept telling Jack, "You are so much better than me at this," and "I'm bad at this stuff." She took a back seat and waited for Jack to give her instructions. But Jack is a really great talker—*not* a great delegator. He took the lead and did most of the work. Jack didn't give Violet much to do. When the pair had to present the project to the class, Violet stood mostly silently while Jack prattled on and on.

Their teacher pulled Violet aside after class and reprimanded her, saying, "Next time, don't leave all the work to Jack, okay?"

In this version of the story, Violet doesn't realize her power. She admits defeat before the project even starts in order to defend herself from feeling stupid. It backfires, though, because the teacher can't see that Violet is struggling with insecurity. He only sees Violet being lazy.

Now let's look at the story as if Violet *did* realize her power.

Violet was assigned to work with Jack on a history presentation. She was happy about the pairing because she knew their team would be strong. Jack had a very good command of history.

Violet thought about what *she* could contribute to the presentation—she was a pretty good public speaker, and it wasn't as though she was *bad* at history, it was just that Jack was kind of exceptional. Together they could learn from each other.

With that attitude, Violet and Jack worked well together. Sometimes he would get on her nerves because he was a know-it-all—but it helped that they had a common goal: to get this thing done and to make it good. When Jack was hogging the whole thing, Violet insisted that she wanted to speak on certain subjects to the class. Jack hadn't realized he was hogging, and he was happy to share the stage. Violet used her public speaking skills to make up for what she didn't know in history. Jack filled in the gaps. Their presentation went very smoothly, and the teacher gave them an A.

Here, Violet accepts that Jack is good at history, but it doesn't make his voice more powerful or more important than hers. She *hones* in on her strengths and stands up for herself. She realizes that she *is* instrumental in making this a good presentation, and she owns it.

BE ACCOUNTABLE, AND HOLD OTHERS TO THE SAME STANDARD

The thing about power is that it comes with responsibility. A Difficult Empowered Bitch embraces this responsibility by being accountable for his own actions. He doesn't go around blaming everyone else for his attitude or behavior. He admits to his part in things, including his mistakes.

However, accountability is not just about owning up when you did something "bad," although that's important too, and it shows strength of character.

Accountability also means following up on promises to others. It means recycling because you are accountable to the environment. It means exercising because you're accountable to your own health—nobody's going to exercise for you, and nobody's stopping you (hopefully). It means that if you're babysitting a kid, you are accountable for that kid. Also, being accountable is a very mature personality trait, which employers and colleges love. Just saying.

Plus, if you're accountable for your actions, you get to hold other people to the same standard. People in your life should keep their promises and do their jobs. If they fail you, they need to make amends.

SPEAK UP

Speak up for yourself and speak up for others. A Difficult Empowered Bitch knows that her voice is important. She doesn't get caught up in petty nonsense, but she uses her voice when it matters. She stands up for her rights and for the rights of others. When she feels empowered and physically safe, she gives bullies the business (nonviolently), or ignores them completely. She tells people what she needs when she is sad or angry. She opens up when things are hard in her life, because she knows that will lead to healing.

SHOULDA COULDA WOULDA

Can you think of a time when you should have spoken up, but you didn't?

Maybe you witnessed something happening to another person, or something happened to you, and you stayed silent or laughed along.

Or perhaps you were going through something difficult, but you told no one even though you really needed the support.

Most people have memories of a time when they shut down in order to get through a tough situation or because they didn't know any better. Don't beat yourself up for not speaking up.

Instead, take your regrets and channel them into empowerment in your future. Perhaps next time, you'll say something. This sort of thing takes practice.

DON'T APOLOGIZE SO MUCH

Obviously, if you've done something messed up, you should apologize. That shows maturity and accountability.

However, it's so common for people, especially women and girls, to apologize ALL THE TIME FOR NO REASON. It's a nervous habit that comes from a bigoted old idea that women, trans, and nonbinary folks are not supposed to speak up or even take up space. Difficult Empowered Bitches do not engage with such silliness.

Don't apologize when . . .

You have basic needs.

Here are phrases to avoid:

- "I'm sorry, can I go to the bathroom?"
- "I'm sorry, I just fell and I could really use a Band-Aid."
- "I'm sorry, but can I have some water?"
- "I'm sorry, but can we turn up the heat? I'm freezing."

You get the idea. You are a human being who is allowed to have needs.

You have bigger needs, or when to negotiate.

It's scary to negotiate or to ask for bigger needs. It's easy to undersell yourself, or to think you're some kind of a burden for asking. But apologizing doesn't help.

Here are some examples of what NOT to say:

- "I don't want to be too much trouble, but I was just hoping to get some extra credit to boost my grade. No worries if not."
- "I'm sorry, but I wanted to talk to you about a problem I'm having in class with some of the comments that people are making that I think are kind of sort of offensive. Is that okay? I don't know if I should be saying anything."
- "I hope it's okay, and I'm sorry to bother you, but I could really use someone to hear me out about what I'm going through right now—if it's not too annoying."

When you use these disclaimers, they diminish something that's obviously very important to you. And for what? To make the other person comfortable? Why would a thousand apologies make the other person more comfortable than asking a direct question? Often these excessive apologies can actually make them feel uncomfortable and awkward, because they might feel pressure to reassure you that everything's fine. So not only are you not helping anyone else feel more comfortable, but you're also not demonstrating the importance of the issue.

On the other hand, don't come in spouting demands and ultimatums either, like "I deserve a better grade and you're going to give it to me." That's not going to get you anywhere.

There's a happy medium here, and that's to come in prepared. If you're negotiating for a better grade, for example, tell the teacher *why* you believe you deserve it. Have actual facts on hand. There's no telling what the other person will do or say, but at least you handled it like a Difficult Empowered Bitch. You can be proud of your negotiating skills.

It's obviously someone else's fault.

Sometimes, we have a strange knee-jerk reaction and say "I'm sorry!" when it's obviously the other person's fault.

If someone else steps on your foot, or if someone accidentally opens your bathroom stall and *you're* the one saying "I'm sorry!" then it's time to make a change!

Just because there's conflict, that doesn't mean it's your fault. You can work it out without apologizing for something you didn't do.

You are trying to get a word in edgewise.

Men are 33 percent more likely to interrupt women than to interrupt men. Women are so used to being interrupted and ignored that it feels as though we're being a burden by simply trying to get a word in. So we say stuff like "I'm sorry, can I just interject and say one thing? Would it be okay if I said a few words?" instead of just saying it.

This goes for all genders and all cultural, racial, and abled identities: do not apologize for being a part of the conversation. A Difficult Empowered Bitch's voice is just as important as everybody else's.

You have a dissenting opinion.
You don't have to apologize for having a different opinion than the people around you. As long as you respect other peoples' opinions, you don't have to say things like "I'm so sorry to say this, but I *think* I *might* have a different take, or whatever." Just state how you feel. The world won't end. Your opinion deserves respect.

And a quick note on language: Maybe you're not always saying "sorry" exactly, but you're still diminishing your own voice. Pay attention to phrases such as "I just," "But I was hoping," "I was wondering if I could," "In my opinion," "Personally, I'm not sure but, I feel like . . ." and so on. Try to edit them out and see what you're left with; hopefully it's a much more confident, clear, and assertive request.

A NOTE FROM SHARON
YOU DON'T NEED A POWER SUIT WHEN YOU HOLD YOUR HEAD HIGH

One of the most empowering things you can do as a human being is to figure out who you are and be that person unapologetically . . . but sometimes, that's easier said than done. You've undoubtedly heard the advice "Just be yourself!" a lot, particularly if you live in a country like the United States. The problem is, it's pretty hard to figure out who you are when you have constant noise in your ear from people who've decided who you should be.

It's harder to just be yourself when the world assigns a label to you—Black, brown, gay, disabled, trans, Muslim, Christian, or others—and stereotypes you based on that label. Whatever that label may be, sometimes it can feel impossible to define yourself when everyone seems to only see you for that one thing. The bottom line? Being a Difficult Empowered Bitch is harder for some of us than it is for others.

But here's what you have to remember: How YOU feel about yourself is more important than how the world sees you. These days, we have this societal picture of an empowered woman: She's a career-driven, body-positive, outspoken, unencumbered, independent badass. That woman is amazing, but she's not the only model of empowerment that exists. She may not be an accessible role model to those of us who come from different cultures, backgrounds, abilities, or identities.

You can be an empowered woman who wears a hijab. You can be an empowered woman who poses topless. You can be an empowered woman who doesn't want children. You can be an empowered woman who chooses to be a stay-at-home mom. You can be an empowered woman who doesn't feel comfortable getting political on social media. You can be an empowered woman who is unemployed. You can be an empowered woman who feels self-conscious from time to time. Empowerment can mean different things to different people—and there are so many factors (be they cultural, familial, personal, or racial) that can influence how closely you align with the image of an empowered woman our society has created.

And, of course, there's the element of choice. You have the right to take all those factors that influence your life, examine them without input from the rest of the world, and figure out how they affect who you are. It's easy for some people to feel totally free of their identities, but for some of us (particularly those of us who are marginalized in some way), those identities inevitably play a big role in who we are. The trick, I've learned, is that they're only part of the whole picture. We aren't defined by things like skin color, religious identity, sexual orientation, disabilities, or gender. Rather, we can allow those things to shape our perspective, to give us empathy, and to round out the way we view ourselves.

If you're a Difficult Bitch who wants to break free from those labels, I hear you. I can't stand when people meet me and within minutes feel the need to ask "where I'm from." I hail from an exotic land called Pittsburgh, Pennsylvania, but no one actually wants to know where I grew up; they want to know why my skin is brown. I wish instead of feeling the need to slap a label on me, they'd get to know me as a person first. I have felt, at many times in my life, the overwhelming pressure of being viewed as a woman of color and nothing more.

That's why I roll my eyes a bit when someone who has never been tokenized preaches about the importance of individuality. It's SO MUCH EASIER to be an individual when you're not constantly bogged down by stereotypes or being placed into boxes you didn't choose. The best advice I can give you is this: You are more than your labels. They may make your journey to empowerment a bit more challenging, but you will get there. You will figure out who you are in every dimension. You will find out you're so much more than the sum of all those labels. You will choose what role your identities play in the big, beautiful, multicolored picture you paint of yourself. And one day you'll realize that you like who you are—a lot. And that, dear reader, is what empowerment is all about.

DON'T STRIVE FOR PERFECTION, STRIVE TO BE YOU

You're not going to get it right all the time. Knowing yourself and making empowered choices is a lifelong journey. Some days you might feel totally empowered and like you're Difficult Bitch #1, but on other days, you might feel defeated and not empowered in the least.

In the end, Difficult Bitches have to strive to be themselves no matter what bumps they meet in the road. Remember that perfection does not exist. Instead of chasing an illusion, embrace yourself and learn as much as you can from your role models and from your mistakes. Empowerment will come.

FINDING YOUR COMMUNITY

A Difficult Bitch has no time for drama or nonsense.

Friendships and romantic partners are supposed to be your support. They're never perfect, but in general, you should *get* about the same amount of love that you *put into* a relationship.

However, it doesn't always work out that way. Sometimes you have to be a Difficult Bitch, even with your friends or the people you date.

This chapter is all about navigating friendships and romantic relationships in proper Difficult Bitch–style.

Set boundaries.

Do you hate it when your friend posts pics of you on social media without your permission?

Do you need your boyfriend to chill on his number of phone calls?

Is your girlfriend trying to control what you wear or who you talk to?

Is your friend always bringing up something embarrassing, and you wish she wouldn't?

Is your boyfriend always trying to get in your pants, and you're not down with that?

It's time to be a Difficult Social Bitch and set some boundaries. This means staying in the relationship but getting the offending person out of your business and off your ass. Setting boundaries is about showing respect for yourself and advocating for your needs.

Setting boundaries comes very naturally to some people, but not to others. It's not an easy thing to do because you're disrupting the day-to-day flow of a relationship in order to speak up.

But this book isn't called *How to Be an Easygoing Bitch*.

If you don't set boundaries, your friend's bad behavior won't stop and you'll only grow more resentful. You may have to step out of your comfort zone and channel that inner Difficult Bitch we talked about. If the relationship means a lot to you, it's very important to set boundaries so that you can continue being close.

Here are some tips.

Be firm.

If you want a friend or partner to stop doing something that makes you uncomfortable or hurts you, which has a more lasting impact?

1. "Stopppp!!! (giggle)"

or

2. "I don't like it when you do that, and I don't want you to do it anymore. Okay? Do you understand that? (Wait for response.) Thank you."

The answer is No. 2!

No. 1 is a common, easy-breezy way to smooth things over, but No. 2 will actually force the person to see that you're serious and force them to listen.

Be clear.

Some people need really clear instructions. They can't read your mind.

For the people who can't take a hint, instead of saying, "Don't call me so much," you can say something like "Call me three times a week, and only after eight o'clock." Not only are you setting a very clear boundary, but you're telling the person that you still want them to call, and that you still want them in your life.

Move on.
Now that you've set a boundary, don't dwell. Don't stew or talk shit. You've done the right thing. Now, let it go and let the relationship run its course.

Expect respect.
You put yourself out there and set your boundary. The least your friends and partners can do is try to respect it. Sometimes people make mistakes, but if they repeatedly, maliciously trample your boundaries, maybe this person shouldn't be in your life.

HYPOTHETICAL

Every time Fiona comes over to Gracie's house, she smokes cigarettes in the backyard. For a while, Gracie tried to be okay with it. But as it turns out, she really, *really* hates the smell. She's also sick of feeling paranoid about her parents finding the butts or smelling the smoke on her clothes.

So one day, when Fiona asked if she could come over after school, Gracie felt anxious. She wanted to make up an excuse to say no.

But instead, Gracie channeled her inner Difficult Social Bitch. She decided she really wanted to stay friends with Fiona, and she loved having her over. But in order to keep the relationship, she'd have to have a difficult conversation.

"Yes, come over! Just one thing, you can't smoke at my place anymore. Okay?"

"Oh. Sorry. Why?" Fiona asked.

"I've been meaning to tell you that I don't like the smell and I don't want my parents smelling it. Maybe you can go down the block. Or just lay off for a few hours? Is that doable?"

"Sure. I think so. I mean, if you don't want me to come over . . . "

"Fiona, you're awesome. I love you and I want you over to my place all the time. I promise it's not deep."

"Okay. No problem. I'll chew gum or something instead."

Gracie set up a boundary without any drama, and Fiona obliged without any drama. Now they can move on. They still get to enjoy their relationship, only now this weight is off Gracie's shoulders. (Hopefully Fiona will eventually quit the habit, but that's another story for a different day.)

FORGET ABOUT POPULARITY

Here's a revolutionary idea: Forget about popularity. Really, forget *all* about it. It's not important. It's mind-boggling how much importance is placed on popularity when you're in school, and how *utterly unimportant* it is in the totality of your life. It is a giant waste of everybody's time and energy, and every single person in your school will realize that very, very soon. (Yes, even Becky.) A Difficult Social Bitch doesn't subscribe to such trivialities in the first place.

You have permission to

- **Be unpopular. You've got way more important stuff to worry about.**
- **Be popular, as long as you don't take yourself too seriously and you use your power for good and not evil, okay?**
- **Stay friends with the uncool kid if she makes you happy and treats you well.**

- **Date the guy from film club if you like him, even though your friends think he's weird.**
- **Say no to the party filled with popular kids if you don't feel like going.**

You get the gist.

If anyone tells you otherwise, they're wrong, plain and simple. You get to be the Difficult Social Bitch who walks away instead of fretting over this nonsense. In a few years, Becky will tell you: "You were so much cooler than all of us because you were yourself."

LISTEN AND SHARE

Some people have an easier time listening than sharing, or vice versa. It's important to try to balance the two so that your friendships aren't one-sided. A Difficult Social Bitch can stop and listen to her friends before chiming in right away. However, she can also share her thoughts, feelings, and struggles. She values the same balance in her friends, because this kind of equality can lead to deeper connections, as opposed to superficial friendships.

STAND UP TO ASSHOLES

There are Difficult Social Bitches, and then there are plain assholes. Assholes are the bullies, the mean girls, the harassers, the slut-shamers, the pushy people, or the folks who make you, or someone else, feel bad on purpose.

A Difficult Social Bitch will stand up to an asshole directly if she can, or she will report the asshole to an adult.

A Difficult Social Bitch will never, *ever* join in on the asshole activity. She's not a complicit bitch.

A Difficult Social Bitch calls people out if they're being cruel, exclusionary, racist, ableist, homophobic, abusive, slut-shaming, or sexist.

A Difficult Social Bitch will never stoop to the asshole's

level. She will not resort to name-calling, cruelty, social media shenanigans, or violence. A Difficult Social Bitch is above all of these easy routes.

SHOULDA COULDA WOULDA

Can you think of a time in your life when you didn't stand up to an asshole, but you should have?

Was there a time when you could have stopped a friend from bullying someone else?

Was there a time when you could have stood up for yourself or reported a behavior to an adult?

Do you remember ever reacting to an asshole in a way that you're not proud of?

Everyone has this kind of memory, or memories. It doesn't make you a bad person, but it's important to remember and reflect on these moments.

Difficult Bitches learn from their mistakes.

KNOW WHEN TO WALK AWAY

Sometimes a Difficult Social Bitch just has to ask herself, Is this relationship worth it?

You can't choose your family, but you *can* choose your friends and the people you date. It might feel as if you're stuck, but you're not.

Here's how to tell if you're in a toxic relationship versus a normal teenage situation. The following applies to friendships as well as dating situations.

A Difficult Social Bitch has no time for toxic relationships.

TOXIC RELATIONSHIP	NORMAL TEENAGE SITUATION
You're unhappy or anxious in the relationship most of the time.	You're unhappy or anxious once in a while.
You feel like you always have to please them, or like you're always walking on eggshells.	Sometimes you disagree or even fight, but neither person has more control than the other.
They repeatedly disregard your boundaries.	They might forget about your boundaries sometimes, but they act cool when you remind them.
They push you into doing stuff you don't want to do, no matter what you say.	They sometimes nudge you or tease you but back off when you're serious.
They need to be in contact with you around the clock, and you're not into it.	Sometimes they can be extra when it comes to texting you, but that's pretty mutual.
They try to get you to hate the important people in your life.	They talk shit sometimes, but they're not really trying to control who you're friends with, or who you love.
They have unreasonable expectations that you'll never be able to meet.	They like it when you're feeling generous and they need you to remember their birthday, but they don't expect the moon from you all the time.
They unload all of their problems on you, and not on anyone else.	They vent a lot, but they also confide in other friends and a counselor.
They routinely make fun of you or belittle you in ways that make you feel bad.	They joke around and tell you to lighten up sometimes, but they back off if you're seriously offended. Besides, it's mutual.
They talk about you behind your back when they're mad at you.	They might confide in someone else when you're fighting, but they don't spread secrets or lies, or try to hurt you.
They don't care about how you feel, at all.	They forget to consider your feelings sometimes, but if you speak up, they'll listen.

Table continued on next page.

Table continued from previous page.

TOXIC RELATIONSHIP	NORMAL TEENAGE SITUATION
They feel entitled to your time and energy, even if you're busy or have a life.	They ask for your help when they need it, and they are disappointed when you're busy — but it ends there.*
They blame you for issues that are obviously their own.	They seek your support to a reasonable degree, and they don't blame you for their own issues.
They get mad or jealous over nothing in order to control you.	They get mad and jealous sometimes, but you confront it and neither of you seeks control over the other.
Things just feel wrong all the time, and you can't quite put your finger on why.	Things feel calm, normal, and right most of the time.
They are violent.	They horse around in a consensual, mutual way.

*In case of crisis:
It's one thing if your friend is having a bad day. It's another if they are having a mental health crisis, physically injured or in danger, or going through a family emergency. It's bad form to abandon a relationship in the middle of a crisis. However, you can't shoulder the burden of healing someone by yourself, and a good friend wouldn't expect that from you. If a friend is unable to get help themselves, refer them to a crisis hotline and tell a guidance counselor, their parents, or a trusted adult in your life who's in a position to take action.

If you're feeling trapped in a toxic relationship, it's time to move on.

BREAK UP SMART

Don't just ghost.

It's tempting to ghost—disappear without texting, calling, or saying a word. It's the easy way out, and once in a while it actually works.

However, a person who's already been treating you badly might ramp up their bad behavior if you ghost, or they might not get the hint. Also, if you have to see them on a regular basis, ghosting will make your life awkward. It's not worth the anxiety.

Plus, a Difficult Social Bitch doesn't hide.

Communicate clearly, firmly, and briefly that you want out.

You don't need to write a Pulitzer-winning text or deliver a tear-inducing speech to get out of a bad relationship. In fact, brevity can be the best way to rip off the Band-Aid and leave without any more drama.

Here are two hypothetical options.

1. **"It's hard to say this, but I am not happy in this relationship. I have given it many chances. Please do not call me or attempt to reconcile. If I see you in the hall, I will nod and keep walking, but that will be the extent of our relationship. Be well, and I really do wish the best for you."**

or

2. **"So, here's the deal. I don't want to hang out with you anymore. I've thought it over and it just isn't right. I am going to tell you what went wrong, so that you don't do it to someone else.**

   - **You call me too much.**
   - **You try to control me.**
   - **You're mean about my appearance.**
   - **When I tell you to stop doing these things, you don't.**

   So you've given me no choice. I have to break off contact with you. Don't try to talk to me, call me, or text me, and don't talk to my friends either.

   I hope you fall off a cliff."

Which one is a better breakup message? No. 1!

Even if No. 2 feels more cathartic, it's a bad choice. You two are past the point of working out your problems, so there's no reason to go into detail. Besides, the list of problems will give the other person an opening to argue. And telling them to fall off a cliff might just engage them more by stoking their anger.

Telling them not to talk to your friends, depending on the situation, might be an unreasonable demand. A Difficult Social Bitch doesn't cause more drama. She walks away from drama with her head high and stays firm. You know how in movies the cool people don't look at the explosions behind them? That's you.

If the idea is to move on from someone cleanly once and for all, No. 1 is a way better choice.

Expect nothing.

Once you've delivered your mic-drop breakup, don't expect anything. The person might get angry. They may not respect your boundaries at first, so you have to hold firm and not answer their texts. They may ask you a thousand questions trying to engage you again. They may apologize, but that apology will likely be insincere and calculated to get you back. Don't expect them to change, as much as you'd like them to.

Stick to your guns and move on. Let them do their own healing. Then you're being a true Difficult Social Bitch.

That said, if someone's toxic behavior is ramping up into stalking, harassing, or violence, it's time to report it to a trusted adult and take out the trash for real.

A NOTE FROM MARY
YOUR PEOPLE ARE OUT THERE

By the time I was a freshman in high school, I had realized I was pretty different from the rest of my peers. I started to feel utterly hopeless that I would ever fit in, let alone be one of those confident popular girls who everyone knew and loved and who all the boys liked. Everyone knew of me; I was the only blind girl in my school. To add to what I considered to be my weirdness, I was a nerd, painfully awkward, and shy. I was different, and the world isn't always kind to different.

Though I was a social outcast in high school, I somehow always found my people, even if we were the vast minority. In high school, my people were all the nerds. My social circle was comprised of literally some of the smartest people I've met—they went on to attend Ivy League colleges and majored in things like astrophysics and cybersecurity. They knew how to hack—which, BTW, is usually illegal, so don't do it—and we bonded over the fact that we were all outcasts, and the kind who did competitive trivia for fun.

Being different allowed me to find my best friend of sixteen years. She started high school as a junior after being homeschooled her whole life. At first glance, it was hard to find what we had in common. I thought she was brilliant, gorgeous, athletic, and, of course, nondisabled. But she also felt like an outcast because she had never been around people her own age in a school setting before.

We were in the same geometry class together, geometry being my archnemesis. At first, I couldn't stand her. While I struggled with deciphering our teacher's solution to a problem, she would always raise her hand and say "Well, I solved it another way," and proceed to baffle me further with an explanation that made even less sense than the original solution.

But then one day we had all brought in kites and had to fly them during class. Well, I was blind, and no one would let me run alone. I had a personal aide who had severe back problems so she for sure wasn't running. I was standing around as usual, feeling like a total loser. My soon-to-be best friend came by and asked if she could run my kite with me. And we did, and we never looked back.

This story could have ended differently. I felt so alone all the time and thought that I wasn't super easy to approach. But she persisted, and I finally allowed myself to be vulnerable enough to let her in. It's easy to shut off and pretend that we don't care when we are afraid of getting hurt and people being unkind to us. However, closing ourselves off completely will mean that we miss out on potential friendships that could last a lifetime.

My life was further changed when I finally met other people my age who were also blind or disabled. We were able to speak about how we felt, how we all had crushes, and how we wanted to have the latest styles. We also talked about how we liked the same celebrities, and how none of us were happy with the way we looked. In short, we were like everyone else, but no one else could see it because they focused too much on our disabilities.

Here's the bad news: Even adults don't deal well with different. There are people who will never overcome their biases and "isms" to know the beautiful person you are. The good news is that you will always find your people.

Being different is hard. As a thirty-year-old, I still find it takes me longer to form true friendships. But that also means that the friendships I make are deeper and, so far, have lasted a lifetime. And yeah, dating as a disabled woman often leaves a lot to be desired, but that isn't a reflection on me—it's a reflection of the flawed and prejudiced society we live in. Plus, being blind and dating is super useful. It's easy for me to filter out a lot of jerks, since if you can't see past a disability to know the great person I am, then I can say "Girl, bye" without wasting time and energy.

Finally, it's okay to struggle with finding your identity, and it's okay to cry sometimes. For me, the key to my social happiness lies in the knowledge that no matter how the world views me, I am talented, valuable, and beautiful. My diversity is a strength. It doesn't matter how much I weigh or how many parties I'm invited to or how many boys like me. What matters is that I know I'm pretty damn awesome, and that there are a few select people who love me when I'm awesome as well as when I'm difficult. There is no such thing as a Difficult Bitch who isn't awesome in her own way.

BEING YOUR FIERCE-ASS SELF

A Difficult Bitch doesn't care what people think.

Okay, that's impossible. Everyone cares what people think, at least a *little*. But within every Difficult Bitch, there is a self-expressive queen (or king or nonbinary royal) waiting to pop out.

That doesn't mean you need to start rocking crowns and gowns to show everyone your self-confidence. Rather, being a Difficult Self-Expressive Bitch means being yourself from head to toe and ignoring the jealous, judgy background noise. It means taking risks on your own terms. It means loving your body, whether you choose to flaunt it or not. It means owning your look, your bod, your intelligence, your music taste, and everything in between. Let's go.

EMBRACE YOUR TASTE

You like what you like, and you don't like what you don't like.

Some things might grow on you, like a song you hated the first time you heard it but has now become your jogging jam. People change sometimes.

It's important to stay open-minded to new experiences

and ideas. But for the most part, it's pretty hard to completely change your visceral likes and dislikes overnight.

So the best thing to do is to be honest with yourself and embrace your taste. Just because a friend likes a jacket, that doesn't mean you have to like it. Or just because a cousin doesn't like your new haircut, that doesn't mean you have to shave it off. You should be able to keep relationships without changing your tastes. If a friend isn't down with that, it might be time to ditch them.

HYPOTHETICAL

All of Casey's friends love Taylor Swift. Casey (who uses they/them/theirs pronouns) tried to get into Swift's music for years. They went to concerts. They bought posters. They gossiped about the singer's love life with their friends, especially Jonna, who is obsessed.

But one day, Casey realized that they had just been forcing themselves to go along to get along. They had to admit that they were never going to truly like Taylor Swift. Definitely not in the way Jonna does.

So Casey took a deep breath and said to Jonna for the first time: "I don't like Taylor Swift. I don't think I ever have."

"Wait. What? How could you not?!" Jonna asked.

"Because she's boring. She makes me feel nothing," said Casey. "Give me hip-hop or something to dance to."

Jonna gasped playfully. "But what about the Jake Gyllenhaal breakup song?"

"It is soooo baaaad," Casey laughed. "Also, there's no proof that it's about Jakeycakes."

"Jakeycakes?!" Jonna grinned. "You did *not*."

It was a wonderful, freeing feeling. Not only did Casey feel as if they were being true to themselves about this issue, but they were also able to have a lively conversation.

LOOK INSECURITY IN THE FACE

If we're being honest, insecurity is real. Insecurity is that feeling that's all like "But . . . is this *really* okay?" or "Does this *really* look good on me?" or "Am I kidding myself?" or "Is everyone secretly making fun of me?" and "I could never pull that off."

Everyone feels it from time to time. Even supermodels feel it (perhaps *especially* supermodels because they're under so much pressure to be perfect). In many ways, society is getting more open-minded about body image and beauty image, but we can't deny that insecure thoughts and feelings still exist. You're not the first and you're not going to be the last Difficult Bitch who second guesses her self-expression.

You can't turn off your feelings. But you can pause, look at those feelings critically, and remind yourself that insecurity doesn't have to be your reality.

If you start to feel insecure, remember the following:

- **You are your worst critic. Nobody cares as much as you do. Everyone else is pretty consumed with themselves. That cellulite dimple you're obsessing over? Just act like nobody notices, because there's a good chance they don't. It's usually a big deal only in your head.**
- **Who are these people again? The people whose opinions matter so much? The random people in your PE class? Your best friends on the beach? That dude you kinda like? Unless these people are going to give you $10 million to be cellulite-free, what does their**

opinion even matter? (You have permission to use
that comeback anytime someone makes a comment.)
After graduation, their opinions will matter even less.

- **If anyone has a problem with your self-expression,
  it's on them, not you. You're not obligated to protect
  people from who you are. You're just living life.**

LOVE YOUR BOD

We spend so much energy fretting about our bodies. Most
people have body issues at some point, and it's almost
impossible to shut it off completely.

So instead, try channeling that worry into self-love. Your
body is a beautiful gift. There is no such thing as a perfect
body—it is your special, one-of-a-kind vessel in this life. Take
care of it. If you want to get or stay fit, that's great—but you
don't have to hate on your body while you do it. Thank your
body every day for the work that it's doing for you. It's your
best buddy in the world.

And as long as you're practicing healthy habits, who cares
what that one model looks like? Or if low-rise jeans aren't your
look? Or if your toes are a little long for flip-flops? These days,
there are wardrobes made for nearly every size and every
taste, abled or disabled. You don't have to wear shorts if you
don't feel like it. But if you really, *really* want to wear shorts
(it's hot out!) and the *only thing* that's stopping you is body
image, that's when it's time to change the channel to self-love.
Your comfort and self-expression are way more important than
some random body standard, no matter what your brain or
silly gossipers are telling you. And anyone who judges you or
dismisses you for your body is not worth your time.

TAKE A RISK

Try taking a risk once in a while. Cut your hair differently—
it'll grow back. Wear weird nail polish—there's always
remover. Try a style for a day that you've never worn before.

Go goth. Go punk. Go basic. Dress like Steve Jobs. Pushing your boundaries can be really liberating, and it'll remind you that expressing your style isn't so serious or permanent.

A NOTE FROM SHARON
LET'S TALK ABOUT HAIR.

Is there anything more politicized than a Black woman's hair? Whether she wears it natural, relaxes it, gets weaves sewn in, or chops it all off in a glorious haze of spontaneity—or any of the million other options our versatile textures open up for us—there are going to be a million and one people who seem to have an opinion about it.

Maybe your family wants you to get a relaxer (or, as your grandma probably calls it, a perm) so that you can look "professional" for college interviews. Maybe your grandma has been on you for looking "a mess" when you go to church. Maybe your friends are really into natural hair care and analyzing their curl patterns and turn up their noses if you still straighten your 'fro sometimes. Maybe your boyfriend wants you to get "boxer braids" like Kim Kardashian, and now you have to break up with him because he's stupid enough to think that "boxer braids" is what the style's called and that Kim Kardashian, a white/Armenian woman, actually invented it.

Hair can feel like a battlefield, one where you have to pick sides, when maybe all you want to do is like the way you look and wear your hair in a way that feels truly, authentically you. But it can be hard to figure out what it is you actually like without factoring in what you think people will think about you. And not to mention that authenticity means something different for everyone.

Hair should be fun, and it can be fun—you just have to learn to quiet the voices around you. Learn to shut down "hair talk" that doesn't serve a positive purpose. "My hair, my choice" should be your mantra, and you have to believe it yourself before you can enforce it when dealing with others. So make inspiration boards on Pinterest or follow a slew of Instagram accounts focusing on the kind of styles that inspire you. (Just be careful about getting too caught up in the fake perfection of social media.)

Ask yourself this: What styles do you see on others that make you automatically feel happy? What styles make you feel the most "you" you can be? What styles make you feel like Beyoncé—like you can take on the entire world and win?

Imagine this: You're the princess of a magical, multicultural, totally nonjudgmental land where you're the sole trendsetter, and there are no rules or expectations regarding your or any other Black girl's hair. What would you do with your hair? Dye it purple? Get box braids in every color of the rainbow? Press your hair until it's sleek and shiny? Or pick out your natural curls until your Afro feels larger than life?

Hair isn't something to be graded on—don't love your natural self any less because you decided to get your hair braided or relaxed or cut all the way off. Have fun with it, and leave everyone else's bullshit at the door.

TAKE MEDIA WITH A GRAIN OF SALT

YouTube, TV, Instagram, magazines—there's a lot going on behind the scenes to create the illusion of reality. You've probably heard that a lot, but it's actually true.

Models and influencers have trainers, dietitians, aestheticians, makeup artists, hairstylists, amazing photo editors, high-end cameras, fabulous lighting, wardrobe experts, surgeons, props, sponsors, and teams of people whose job it is to make these humans look flawless. They are beautiful, sure, but *nobody* looks top-notch fantastic all the time without those kinds of resources. When companies want to sell something, they will stop at nothing to exploit your insecurities and create fantasies. It's an expensive illusion.

Models devote their careers to their looks, so they're amazing at looking a certain way. If they devoted all of their time to other pursuits, they'd be amazing at that instead. Whatever you decide to devote *your* life to, you will be excellent at it, and you have incredible value to this world. But know that, just like every other field, being "visually perfect" is a lot of work.

Being a Difficult Self-Expressive Bitch means taking media with a grain of salt. It means seeing these images and videos for what they are. That's not to say that you shouldn't enjoy the beauty of Beyoncé or Margot Robbie, but unless you plan to commit to their lifestyles, look for some role models from your real life.

A NOTE FROM SHARON
ON PERSONAL STYLE

Insecurity about standing out—we've all felt it, but it can hit especially hard when you're the lone Black girl in a sea of faces that don't necessarily look like yours, and you don't know what to expect. There may be that voice in your head nagging you to do whatever you can, however you can, to be less—less loud, less noticeable, less Black. (Does this voice sound like your aunt, who may have self-hating issues of her own? Or maybe it sounds like someone who judged you when you were young, whom you believed because you didn't know better.) But being who you are isn't a bad thing.

Your hair, whether it stands straight up like a gravity-defying crown or flows over your shoulders making you look like the queen you were born to be, isn't something to be ashamed of. Your skin, and the way your bright lipstick pops against your melanin, may stand out in a crowd, but that doesn't mean you should hide it.

You may be afraid to be noticed because you don't want to be noticed for the wrong reasons. You may be afraid that people are already judging you as soon as they see you, even though you haven't even said a word or interacted with them. This feeling, this fear, may seem like something that isn't spoken about a lot, especially if you don't have a lot of Black friends or family you can talk openly with. But it's something that many, many Black people—Black women especially—struggle with when they're in spaces where they may be the only brown face in the room.

This feeling can cause anxiety. What if people think I don't belong? What if they think I'm only here because our dance teacher wanted the team to look diverse? What if they think I'm just the token Black friend and no one at this party really likes me or wants me here?

Feeling like all eyes are on you can be a terrifying experience, and as tempting as it may be to shrink away in the hopes that you can somehow just look like everyone else, Difficult Bitches fight the urge to lessen themselves in the face of a few stares, and instead stand proudly wherever they are. It's not up to you to disprove or even think about any negative stereotypes that may spring to someone's mind when they see you.

Say you've got a new part-time job or internship, but you also treated yourself to a daring new acrylic manicure the day before. Will your new coworkers think you're unqualified, or—gasp—ghetto? This is a word that haunts many Black women when it comes to making personal styling choices. Will this hair color make me look ghetto? This nail color? This lipstick? Will being myself damn me to a lifetime of being looked down on and judged by people who don't care to get to know me?

We're implicitly taught that ghetto is the worst thing you can be, without being similarly taught that beliefs on what counts as "ghetto" (which is synonymous with being not smart, incapable, or unworthy—all classist things!) are heavily influenced by racism. For instance, why is it that when the white lead singer of your favorite band dyes her hair pink, she's a rebel and a badass, but when a dark-skinned woman does it, people may turn their nose up at her? The same can be said of piercings, tattoos, or any outfit that's not khakis and a crisp, plain button-down in an inoffensive, neutral color. Bold style choices can be perceived differently when brown and black skin is involved, but that doesn't mean you have to be any less stylistically daring than your heart desires.

There's no one way to be Black. You don't have to dress like a young Michelle Obama or Kerry Washington in *Scandal* if you don't want to (although, if you do, more power to you! Rock those stylish power suits, girl!). You're allowed to experiment with your appearance, and however you decide to decorate yourself doesn't make you any less smart or less anything (except for less afraid of other people's judgment), no matter what anyone says. If you're ever made to feel like that—and it may happen, especially in a professional setting or around strangers—well, that's a good time to flex the old "I don't give a damn" muscle. Practice picking out the criticism you can actually use and grow from and throwing away other people's expectations of what the "right" kind of Black girl looks like.

Example of helpful feedback: "That skirt may be too short for your part-time job if it's in an office. What are you technically allowed to wear in your office setting?" Example of unhelpful advice that 100 percent is coming from a hater: "That skirt makes you look like you're 'fast.'"

So put on that fuchsia eyeliner you bought two weeks ago but have been too scared to wear outside of your bathroom. The same goes for that blood-red lipstick that makes you feel like a superpowered, pop-star assassin—makeup should be fun, and it's for everyone, and anyone who thinks that Black girls shouldn't wear certain colors or styles because it "doesn't look right" can go jump off a cliff. Not caring what people think is easier said than done, but it's like a muscle that gets stronger and stronger every time you look in the mirror and decide you like what you see, regardless of what the outside world may have to say about it.

Keep working out that muscle, no matter how nervous you get, or how scary it feels to wear that skirt or that hairstyle or that lipstick. The fact is, you may always stand out in some way, if you're the only Black girl at your school, on your dance team, or in your film club. And that's okay! Blending in is overrated, and maybe you were born to stand out. Cliché? Maybe. But it's true. Remember, it doesn't matter what anyone else thinks—as long as you can look in the mirror and smile, then you're on to something.

IGNORE THE GOSS

There is nothing more beautiful and intimidating than a Difficult Bitch who doesn't care about gossip. Nothing puts a judgy or jealous person in their place more than dismissing their opinion entirely, without even being mean back.

Remember that people who gossip or talk smack are facing insecurities in their own lives. Disarm them with a compliment. Tell them how smart or pretty they are. The surprised look on their face will be priceless.

Here are other things you can say:

"Don't be jealous."

"You know I look good."

"I wish you the absolute best in life."

Or just walk away like you can't even hear them.

SHOULDA COULDA WOULDA

Can you think of a time earlier in your life when somebody said something mean to you?

Got one?

Think about your reaction. Maybe it upset you a lot at the time. Maybe you let it get to you. And now, looking back, it's not such a big deal. Maybe you can even laugh about it.

At the end of the day, who cares what that person thought or said? It has no effect on your life right now. You're stronger. Wiser.

Imagine if you could have that attitude toward gossipers *right now*. Because in a few years, or even days, the sting will wear off and you'll be able to laugh about it. You're on a train toward empowerment and being the best *you* possible—if they're not about that, they need to get off your train.

SUPPORT OTHER DIFFICULT SELF-EXPRESSIVE BITCHES

If you're going to be a Difficult Self-Expressive Bitch, you have to support your fellow sisters-in-Bitchitude. If you see someone making a self-expressive choice—be it related to fashion, body, beauty, whatever—you need to support them.

Even if their expression is not your taste *at all*, that person is taking a risk, which is super admirable. Give them a high five. Defend them against gossipers. Trade Difficult Self-Expressive Bitch tips. Find your community and own the halls squad-style.

(The exception is anything hate-based. You are under no obligation to support someone who chooses hateful clothes or lifestyles—in fact, report them to an adult immediately. And if someone is taking fashion cues from a culture they're not closely connected to, you might want to gently suggest that they reconsider.)

RECOGNIZE WHEN "BITCH" IS MISUSED

We've been taking it for granted that *bitch* can be an empowering word. But a lot of people still use the word negatively, whether to put down women or emasculate men. Some people live in more misogynistic settings than others. A lot of people in power—including politicians—still use the word in a nasty way.

If you hear the word used in a bad way, use your judgment. You might fight back by educating the person verbally about the meaning of the word "bitch," if it feels safe and worth your time. You might decide to rise above and ignore the statement. Or you might think bigger and try to change the culture through activism. But also remember that you're not obligated to fight every battle. You're only one person, and you only have so many places to expend your energy.

But no matter what, don't just accept that the way they're using the word is right.

GET HELP

If you're being bullied—which is different than dealing with petty gossip—tell a trusted adult. Get it handled.

If you're having issues with body image, insecurity, and self-expression, professional help is an option. Experts estimate 10 to 20 percent of children and teens may experience mental health issues, including eating disorders, anxiety, and depression. Sometimes teens aren't struggling with these issues but still need someone to talk to. Guidance counselors, therapists, and social workers are trained to guide you through these problems. You're not alone.

A NOTE ON SAFETY

As long as you're not hurting anyone, you should be able to express who you are without fear for your safety, period.

Unfortunately, the world does not always agree. Some self-expressions might incite bullies to mess with you. For example, gender-nonconforming clothing might get a few homophobes in a tizzy. Or a greedy person might be looking for a shiny, expensive coat to steal.

You may worry that if you choose *not* to be fully yourself in a given situation, that means the bullies win. After all, isn't it better to stick up for who you are, regardless of your safety? Isn't the risk worthwhile for the greater good?

Actually, the greater good doesn't want you to get hurt. Your safety is of the utmost importance, and anyone supporting causes for justice and making the world a better place will agree. If you can't safely express yourself the way you want, you can participate in activism (see chapter 9) to change the problems that made you unsafe in the first place.

So, practice good judgment. Use your support system. And if anyone uses violence or abuse against you, remember that it's *not your fault.* Report their actions to an adult right away. If a Difficult Bitch can't express herself, she fights for her right to do so—safely.

EMBRACING YOUR INNER GODDESS

Since chapter 3 got us focused on loving our bodies, let's take it further and talk about health, fitness, and mindfulness. You might be forced to run laps in gym class, but in the end, *you* are the only person who can make yourself fit, healthy, and mindful overall. A Difficult Healthy Bitch takes accountability for her fitness, which means she'll take care of herself—and treat herself.

When I say fit and healthy, I do *not* mean trying to attain some imagined ideal body type. Remember that bodies come in all different shapes, sizes, and abilities. In this book, we're talking about wellness: sustainable ways to build your physical and mental well-being while eating a balanced diet that fuels your body.

THE OBSESSION WITH A PERFECT BODY

Very few people go through their lives without saying, "I wish my body was more like . . ."

But it's concerning if you obsess over your body on a daily basis, if you starve yourself or binge and purge, if you work out compulsively, or if you throw yourself into every fad diet. These might be symptoms of an eating disorder, and you should talk to a doctor if you find yourself doing any of these things.

Much of the world is obsessed with having an extremely skinny or jacked body. If you obsess over your body, it will never bring you peace, no matter how it changes as a result of your obsessions.

If you're having negative thoughts about your body, notice those thoughts. Call them what they are: negative thoughts. Recognizing this will help you avoid spiraling into despair. Then move away from these thoughts and try an exercise in gratitude for your body. Say: "I am so grateful that my body has carried me so far, and I am going to nurture it in return." Then thank the specific body parts you were thinking negatively about. If you feel that you hate your hips, take a moment to thank them for helping you stand up, carry things, or simply keep your balance. If you hate your skin, thank it for protecting you.

SHOULDA COULDA WOULDA

Think about how much time and mental energy you spend putting down your body or feeling anxious about it.

Calculate it. Go ahead. How many times do you spend per hour, per day, per week, and per year putting your body down?

Imagine if, instead, you did something you loved during that time. Imagine if you meditated, walked in nature, took care of your family dog, painted, contributed to a cause, or went for a jog.

The next time you're feeling down on your body, remember that calculation. Give yourself permission to set your negative thoughts aside and focus on something else for a while. You may find that after you've consciously taken a break from self-criticism, those thoughts don't feel as urgent or as valid anymore.

A NOTE FROM SHARON
THE DANGEROUS RELATIONSHIP BETWEEN BODY IMAGE AND HEALTH, OR "IS A THICC ROSE BY ANY OTHER NAME JUST AS FAT?"

Maybe you have your mother's hips, your grandmother's sizable chest, or the dipping and winding curves that all the women in your family have. It can feel as if your body doesn't fit in by anyone's standards. If you started puberty early, how you naturally look can lead to relatives claiming that you're trying to be "too grown," while you feel like your non-Black friends think you're fat because that's how they describe other girls who look like you.

Or maybe you don't have those features. Maybe you get teased for not having the stereotypical "Black girl attributes" that are somehow simultaneously judged harshly and seen as the ideal (but only in some contexts, like when a big butt isn't attached to a big or Black woman). Having people tell you that you're too flat, as if your body somehow makes you less Black, can feel just as crappy.

In either scenario, it can be hard to separate perceived beauty and cultural standards from your actual health. But fear not—even Michelle Obama has struggled with body image issues. Being healthy and exercising does not have to get tangled up in either downplaying or building up whatever features you already have. You're not obligated to do a million squats a day because Black girls are "supposed to" have big butts. You're also not obligated to go on an unhealthy diet and try to shrink your hips because your aunt saw you in a swimsuit at a birthday party one time and decided that you dressed too sexy for your age.

Ignore the fads and the ways that body types seem to go in and out of style. Your health is about one person: you. Don't let the world's stereotypes dampen what can be a rewarding hobby. Find a type of exercise that you like, one that gets your blood pumping, and if you insist on squatting, just make sure you have your priorities and reasons in order. And maybe leave the laxative tea and waist trainers alone, which can actually cause damage if you don't know what you're doing.

And just because it needs to be said: Black girls struggle with eating disorders too. Mainstream representation of disorders like bulimia and anorexia tend to show conventionally attractive white girls and women who are, by society's standards, already thin but dying to be thinner. What isn't discussed as often is the fact that those who suffer from eating disorders don't all look the same, and the ideal body that they are told to strive for may vary greatly, depending on that person's culture. Black girls may face outside pressure to have lighter skin in addition to a smaller body, and the "ideal" body may be bigger in some places and smaller in others, leaving girls struggling to mold a Coke bottle physique that's skinny-but-not-too-skinny and thick-but-not-fat. It's exhausting, doubly so because it's rarely talked about in mainstream media. Whether you feel as though you're supposed to look like a video vixen or a ballerina, it's still an impossible game that can't be won.

Listening to yourself rather than outside voices when it comes to eating healthy is a good skill to practice as well. Remember, it doesn't matter if your cousin accuses you of being bougie because you like drinking kale smoothies for breakfast. Perhaps he will soon discover that smoothies are the breakfast choice of champions.

FITNESS 101

Getting fit is all about having the right information. Fad diets and exercise trends come and go, but the core principles of health and fitness remain the same.

Move your body.

Aim for at least thirty minutes a day, every day. Ideally, make your week a combo of moderate aerobic activity (like walking or swimming), vigorous activity (like jogging), and strength training (like lifting weights). Exercising can uplift your mood, give you more energy throughout the day, help you sleep, and improve your focus. Stretch to increase flexibility.

Fuel your metabolism.

Try to exercise or eat breakfast as soon as you wake up in the morning to kick-start your metabolism, which is like your internal "go juice." Your metabolism keeps you fueled and alive. Thanks, metabolism!

Your metabolism changes a lot, depending on what you're putting into your body and when. If you have a fast metabolism, it may be because you're eating consistently all day, and burning off those calories in an efficient way. This makes your metabolism a well-oiled machine. So instead of eating three really big meals, try eating healthy snacks throughout the day to keep your fuel going.

Also, vitamins are *not* a replacement for vital calories, studies recommend food over supplements in most cases.

Eat well.

Here's the general formula of healthy eating: choose whole foods whenever you can, and read nutrition labels to watch for things like added sugar, added salt, and ingredients you don't recognize so you know what you're putting in your body. Eating well will lead to more sleep and more energy— it's all fueling the same machine.

Don't freak out or obsess over these guidelines, though. They are there to guide choices, not make the ultimate decision for you. For some people, it requires a massive lifestyle change, and your family may not support it or understand it—which is challenging if they're buying the groceries. But you can take small steps, such as adding some leafy greens to your breakfast or lunch.

A Difficult Healthy Bitch is always trying to educate herself. Look at labels and get a sense of which ingredients and nutrients foods contain. They will probably surprise you.

The more you get in the habit of choosing healthier options, the more natural it will start to feel. But give yourself a break from time to time. For many of us, life wouldn't be worth living without the occasional piece of cake.

Speak to a nutritionist or general practitioner if you're changing your diet and especially if you have special dietary conditions like celiac disease, Crohn's disease, food allergies or intolerances, or thyroid issues.

Talk to the pros.

If you are making significant changes to your lifestyle, work with a nutritionist and personal trainer to make it happen. And remember to set goals that are in line with your abilities and your body type. I have short legs, for example—always have and always will. My goals should reflect that. Experts can help you set achievable and healthy goals for your body.

SLEEP!

Sleep is critical to fitness and health. Without good sleep habits, everything else crumbles. Read on for more info about sleep.

Avoid fake info.

Your doctor is the most reliable source for health information. If you're looking online, stick to sites that end in .gov or .edu, or sites that are directly related to a health institution, such as MayoClinic.org. As a baseline rule, all articles must be written by a health expert whose credentials are clearly stated.

HYPOTHETICAL

Amy wanted to be skinny with a big butt. She ran every day, did squats, and looked at influencers on Instagram as inspiration.

The activity got her in shape, but she couldn't seem to achieve her ideal body. She still thought she had a flat butt, and in her mind, she still had a belly. Everyone else told Amy that she looked great, but she just didn't see it in the mirror.

She started to eat healthier and work out three days a week. She ate lots of protein and if she wanted to eat something like a burger, she'd add spinach. She only ate dessert once a week. She believed she would decrease her belly fat and increase her butt.

Instead, her legs grew more muscled. Her waist shrunk but never became the washboard she wanted. Amy was upset at first, but then she realized that she had more energy during the day. She had way more strength to carry her toddler brother around. She felt better overall. She started seeing a counselor about her body image. She stopped worrying about the details and accepted her shape, which was serving her so well. Her body brought her joy instead of shame.

Many years later when Amy looked back at photos of herself at the time, she couldn't believe she *ever* hated her body. She saw herself playing soccer with groups of friends and smiling at Halloween parties. All of these wonderful things were happening around her—why had she only focused on her body type?

By committing to taking care of herself, Amy did pretty freaking awesome.

A NOTE FROM SHARON
MENTAL HEALTH, OR "NO, GRANDMA, PRAYER CAN'T FIX EVERYTHING."

For many in the Black community, you've either experienced or heard of someone experiencing an elder describing prayer as a magical cure-all. Haven't wanted to get out of bed in six months? Pray about it. Harming yourself? Pray about it. Thinking seriously about doing something you can't take back? No, really, just pray about it, and maybe have your mom break out the holy oil.

Luckily, those attitudes are going out of style, and mental health is being discussed in the Black community more openly than ever (thanks in part to social media). Still, if others don't understand, or even criticize, your mental health treatment, remember that you are the one who has to live with your health—not them—and no one knows what it's like inside of your head except for you. You wouldn't hesitate to rest if you had a stomachache or to get a cast to set a broken bone, so don't let outdated ideas jeopardize what you know is best for your mental health and personal well-being.

Mental health treatment may still be taboo in some circles, but you can be the one to change that in your family and in your community by speaking up.

MINDFULNESS 101

People love to talk about mindfulness on social media, often in a post including pictures of sunsets on Instagram. If that's your jam, great. Looking at a sunset is a great way to be mindful. But being mindful can happen in any setting, and it can be a very private experience. You don't have to share it with the universe. A Difficult Healthy Bitch knows how to be alone sometimes.

Being mindful means living consciously, or with awareness. People practice mindfulness by meditating, walking in nature, practicing yoga, and more.

Most of the time, our brains are living in the past or the future. We're wondering: What's on my to-do list? What should I say to my friend on the phone? How am I supposed to afford that dress? What if I get this answer wrong on the test?

Our brains are also often busy experiencing memories, good or bad. You're thinking about what your parents said before you left the house today, or you're remembering that a friend treated you poorly last week.

This isn't bad. This is being human. It's how our brains are wired to function. It would be impossible to live without thinking about the past or future.

However, there is one time frame that we often forget to embrace: the present. Living in the present is challenging and takes practice, but it's essentially the goal of being mindful: to be exactly where you are, and *no more.* Being mindful, you focus inward on your spiritual core instead of outward on your social pressures. Sure, some thoughts pop up—such as that drama with your ex—but you can let those thoughts float away. You forgive yourself and everyone else, just for a while, and eventually, more and more. With enough mindful practice, you can temporarily transform yourself into a centered body that is one with the present, instead of a human who wants money or who gets good grades or who needs to impress others or who hates her hips. Instead, you can feel grateful for what you have in this moment and let material issues fall away. Then you can think back to your practice anytime you start to feel anxious or self-loathing.

Being mindful for a short period of time every day can

lead to better health and overall calm, which is what you need in high school more than anything.

Try some popular mindfulness methods.

Meditation

Meditation is a way to get deep into mindfulness. Typically, you start by staying still and focusing on your breath.

Here is a beginner lesson from mindfulness expert Georgina Miranda:

1. Find a quiet space to sit (you can sit in a chair if you like) with a straight spine; let your arms rest comfortably beside you.
2. Close your eyes gently.
3. Start to focus on your breath.
4. Notice how your belly expands as you breathe in and how it comes closer to your body as you breathe out.
5. Maybe place your hand on your stomach to connect better with your body and breath.
6. Breathe at your own rhythm.
7. If thoughts are still cluttering your mind, let them pass by, without judgment.
8. As best you can, focus on your breath and this beautiful moment.
9. Go through five to ten breath cycles.
10. When you are ready, open your eyes.

Don't beat yourself up if you start thinking about a test or the upcoming political election or your next haircut during meditation. It's normal for these thoughts to come in. Just acknowledge each thought, and then recenter your focus on your breath or on a beautiful dot behind your eyelids. A Difficult Healthy Bitch knows how to find peace. Or at least how to try.

Yoga

Yoga is a form of mindful movement and exercise. There are many different kinds of yoga with different levels of intensity, but the practice usually involves a series of poses and stretches and some meditation.

When people start yoga, they may fumble through the poses and feel a bit silly about the whole thing. Over time, though, they may start to get stronger and more flexible, and then they can deepen their experience.

Yoga isn't supposed to be competitive or ego-crushing. Thoughts like "I suck at yoga" aren't relevant in the practice. While you can have fun challenging your body, yoga is all about going at your own pace and listening to your body's needs. You don't have to compare yourself to others so much as tune in to yourself. In fact, yoga is proven to help people work through trauma by connecting them to their bodies in a loving way.

Being in nature

It's great to go out into nature if you can. Hiking and camping are great ways to do this, but when these activities aren't possible, going to a small local park or just finding a tree to sit near can be helpful. Mindfulness is sort of like a return to nature. By being in the present, we can appreciate the body we're in, the ground we're on, the oxygen we're breathing, and the colors we see. Being in nature can help you deepen these feelings. Many people practice mindfulness just by being in nature and focusing on its sights, sounds, and smells.

Getting back to the real world

You can't meditate all the time. Most of us can't do homework or make plans with friends in a meditative state. However, the more you practice mindfulness, the more you'll be able to integrate its principles into tough, real-life situations.

A NOTE FROM SHARON
ON FITTING IN IN HEALTH AND FITNESS SPACES

Never be afraid to try something new or go to a new place. Sure, you may be the only Black girl there—or you may not. Either way, new places are good opportunities to make new friends that you may not have met otherwise.

There are also fitness spaces specifically for Black girls and women to gather, work out together, and promote healthy habits in our communities. Check out groups like Black Girls Run if you're looking for community. Whether you're interested in trying yoga, rock climbing, hiking, or any other fitness activity, chances are there's a group of Black women already doing it together, and who will welcome you with open arms. Try searching local meetup groups for the activity of your choice with the words "Black girl" in front of it and follow people like body-positive yoga goddess Jessamyn Stanley on social media for good vibes and inspiration.

EMBRACING KNOWLEDGE

A Difficult Bitch loves knowledge and learning because they give her more power in the world. Being a Difficult Scholarly Bitch means embracing the worldly learner inside of you and soaking up as much as you can.

Of course, it also means dealing with school, which is no picnic. This chapter isn't a "how-to" on getting good grades. You probably get enough lectures about that in your life, and by now, you understand how important it is.

You also know from chapter 1 that Difficult Bitches are accountable for their own actions, which include school performance. You know the drill: study, go to class, do your homework, and get to the finish line.

But being a Difficult Scholarly Bitch is about more than that. It's about standing up for your education, taking risks, asking for help, and walking through those school doors every day knowing that you belong there and deserve the best.

DON'T SAY, "I CAN'T"

Everyone has strengths and weaknesses when it comes to school. By now, you probably know which subjects come easily to you and which ones you struggle with. However, anytime you say, "I can't," it's usually not true. "I can't do math," "I can't do laps in gym," "I can't make art"—for a Difficult Scholarly Bitch, these are cop-outs. You can do whatever you want if you feel like putting in the work and pushing past the hurdles.

So, instead of language like "I can't," try "I wasn't interested in pursuing it," or "I wanted to focus on other subjects." It shows more empowerment, and it's also closer to the truth. Or even better, you can say, "I'm going to give it a shot."

SHOULDA COULDA WOULDA

Think of a school subject that you struggle with. Maybe you've gotten less-than-stellar grades in this subject, or maybe it just feels really hard. Do you often say "I can't" or "I suck at . . . " when you talk about this subject?

Instead, try to reframe it.

Maybe you took a class and it felt very difficult, but instead of getting the extra help you needed, you gave up on the class.

The next time you find yourself saying, "I can't," try saying, "This is hard, but who can I ask for help?" or "How can I find more time to study?"

A Difficult Scholarly Bitch has accountability and agency in her schooling.

DON'T BE AFRAID TO BE A BEGINNER

It may not feel like a wonderful opportunity now, but high school is filled with incredible learning privileges that you might not get later in life. It can provide the chance to take a class that's a little "off-brand" for you. Maybe you're a science person, but you're a little curious about poetry. Maybe you've been immersed in Mandarin Chinese for ages, but you've always wanted to dabble in French. Unless it's an advanced class, you probably don't need experience to take the class, just a good attitude. Take a risk! It's not a life sentence.

A NOTE FROM MARY
YOU'RE MORE THAN A REPORT CARD

Though I'm a blind Latina, I was very privileged in my education during elementary and middle school. It wasn't until the age of thirteen that I felt the sting of discrimination and truly understood how others' prejudices, stereotypes, and misconceptions not only hurt me emotionally but also compromised the pursuit of my dreams.

Up to eighth grade, I attended schools where most of the students looked like me. All my teachers spoke Spanish, and all my peers were Latinx and of the same socioeconomic status. One of the many advantages of this was that even though I was blind and needed an individualized education plan (IEP), my mother did the really hard advocacy work. She was able to speak up at every meeting and make sure that I was being held to the same academic standard and fulfilling my potential regardless of my disability.

Fast-forward to eighth grade. We moved to the suburbs in New Jersey, and all of a sudden, the demographics changed dramatically. Most of my peers were white. None of the professionals who would be in charge of carrying out my IEP spoke Spanish, so my mom could not communicate as well with them without translation. But we were not too worried—my mother and I trusted "the system" and thought my education would just pick up where we left off.

But on the first day of school, things were not right. I was immediately baffled; all my classes were for the standard track, not the advanced or gifted and talented track as they should have been. I spent a whole day bored in class after class, as I'd already learned all the material being taught at least a year previously. My boredom soon turned into frustration. I had a pretty good idea of what had happened. Even though my new school had my transcript from my other school, which showed basically straight As in honors-level classes for the past two years, they had decided that because I was blind that couldn't possibly be right and that I didn't belong in G&T. I went home that day with a deep feeling that an injustice had been committed against me. I was angry, disappointed, and indignant. That evening, my mom impressed upon me that this time I needed to advocate for myself. She had my back 100 percent, but because of the language barrier, I had to take charge and communicate clearly what the problem was and what needed to happen. Her trust that I could start fighting my own battles strengthened my conviction.

The next day, I walked into the guidance counselor's office. I asked why exactly I was being put in an educational track that was clearly slowing down my learning. She basically told me that I was blind (gasp!) and that I needed to start at a slower pace. That this was a new school and that things here were "different." I had to remind myself to remain calm. The next couple of days I continued to advocate for myself. Eventually my mom did have to come in to help, pointing out certain legalities the school was ignoring or violating, and I was put back on track with the courses I should have been taking to begin with.

Being a Difficult Scholarly Bitch with a disability is challenging, especially if you're also marginalized on the basis of race, gender, or socioeconomic status. Systematic biases and prejudices lead others to try preventing you from succeeding. But academics do not measure your intrinsic value, your kindness, or your humanity, so do not allow things like grades to dictate how you feel about yourself. Recognize that current pedagogical systems are often standardized with a specific person in mind, and that person isn't a woman, a Latina, or blind.

Being a Difficult Scholarly Bitch means I don't need a grade to tell me what I'm good at. My superpower as a Difficult Scholarly Bitch comes from knowing myself, my worth, and my strengths, and ultimately in being able to recognize the same in others so that I can work with them to deliver real-world results. After all, a huge reason why we go to school is that we need a job, and after a certain point, grades don't matter as much. What you know about yourself and how you leverage your strengths matter much more.

FORGIVE FAILURES AND LEARN FROM THEM

Nobody goes through life without failing. It's impossible. Failure isn't even necessarily a bad thing—it makes people interesting and helps them grow. When a Difficult Scholarly Bitch fails at something in school, she feels sad and disappointed, but she knows that it's not the end of the world. Then, instead of moping, giving up, and blaming others, she learns from that failure and uses it to improve her performance. This is an important life skill, not just a high school thing.

FOCUS ON IMPRESSING YOURSELF MORE THAN OTHERS

Impressing friends, family, and teachers is something we all strive to do. But in the end, you'll be a much more confident Difficult Bitch if you listen to your scholarly instincts instead of worrying about everyone else. Take the class that *you* want to take, even if it's not the one all of your friends are taking, for example.

HYPOTHETICAL

(Based on a true story—okay, confession: this actually happened to me.)

I was a huge people pleaser in high school. Frankly, we didn't have books like this one. Girls were expected to get good grades and behave—and for the most part, I did. Teachers loved me. I was NOT a Difficult Bitch in high school, and I regret it deeply.

One teacher didn't like me, though. I'll call her Mrs. Plunk. She taught health and sex ed.

On the first day of class, Mrs. Plunk chose three favorite students—and I was not one of them. Whenever I spoke in class, she seemed to drift off and not listen. Sometimes she even responded to my input derisively.

For example, I did my final project on the *Kama Sutra*, the famous ancient Indian book on sex and eroticism (it was sex ed class after all). I'd worked hard on it. As I presented my work, Mrs. Plunk openly made fun of me in front of the class. "You chose to report on the *Kama Sutra* because it's *all about sex*!" she said.

I was so confused. Wasn't this sex ed class? The presentation did not go well. I was completely derailed and humiliated.

When two of her favorite students presented their team report on incorrect condom usage, Mrs. Plunk said it was a brilliant project and that the students had a "great vibe." (Isn't condom usage all about sex too?)

I tried all semester to make Mrs. Plunk like and respect me. I smiled a lot, I showed unbridled enthusiasm, and I worked way too hard on my homework. Yet she never liked me, and in the end, she gave me a B or something—maybe a C. Who cares?

(Spoiler alert: I survived.)

Here's where it gets weird, though.

When I talked about it with friends later, they all had the same story. In *every class*, Mrs. Plunk chose a few favorites on the first day, then derided everyone else for the entire semester. Later, long after I graduated, students could anonymously rate their teachers online. For fun, I looked up Mrs. Plunk. Guess what? All the reviews of her said the *same thing.*

Turns out, I wasn't doing anything wrong.

I'll never know why Mrs. Plunk behaved the way she did. But I do know now that I wasted my time trying to please an unpleasant person, and I probably should have channeled that effort into reporting her to the administration. What she said to me was absolutely inappropriate and maybe could have even gotten her fired.

Besides, if you ask me, my *Kama Sutra* report was fantastic. I learned a lot in spite of my teacher. In the end, at least I impressed myself.

Don't waste time trying to impress others. *Be you. Impress you.* If they're not impressed with you, they might be a total weirdo like Mrs. Plunk.

A NOTE FROM MARY
ON DISABILITY RIGHTS IN K-12

Some tips on succeeding academically: First and foremost, know your rights. You are covered by the Individuals with Disabilities Education Act (IDEA) through your high school graduation or the age of twenty-two, whichever is earlier. This law guarantees that the school must help you identify and evaluate a disability, and work with you and your parents to develop an individualized education plan. That plan has to be carried out in the "least restrictive environment"—in other words, in the environment that will ensure optimizing your learning. Be warned that many schools unfortunately forget this part of IDEA and put all students with any disability in the same classroom, completely disregarding their learning potential.

Second, lead your IEP meetings! If you need an advocate or expert to help you out, there are organizations that will send out IEP advocates to support you and your parents during these meetings. It's scary to speak up for the first time in a room full of adults who may be patronizing or doubt you, but it's the best time to find your voice. Once you go into postsecondary education, such as college or a trade school, you will not have the protection of IDEA. Instead, you will be covered by the Americans with Disabilities Act (ADA) and section 504 of the Rehabilitation Act, which forces you to be the proactive one rather than the school. High school is good practice for learning how to stand up for yourself. Plus, it's scarier not to get the education you deserve!

Third, know what you want and need out of your education. I was extremely goal-oriented; I wanted to be in all AP classes, I wanted to get into top colleges, and I wanted to excel. But those were my goals—they don't have to be your goals. Not everyone is college bound. Perhaps you want to go to beauty school or art school, or be a plumber, electrician, carpenter, or some other cool and lucrative vocation. Figure out what you want, and go from there. Being a Difficult Scholarly Bitch means that we leverage school and teachers and everything that comes with an education to pursue our dreams. And yeah, I literally have never used the Pythagorean theorem in my professional life, but I had to know that shit when I was testing to go into business school. And I promise that in the business world, there's no geometry—but a little geometry never hurt anyone. Well, not permanently. So, Difficult Scholarly Bitches, go forth and take control of your education and don't let others' low expectations stop you.

YOU HAVE RIGHTS

It may not feel as if you have rights when you're stuck taking a three-hour standardized test. However, all students have rights—like, bona fide legal ones.

In public schools, you have . . .

The right to be accommodated.

Mary talks about this in important detail on page 76. Generally, all students have a right to an education. The Americans with Disabilities Act says teachers and administrations *must* accommodate you regardless of your socioeconomic or disability status and give you all the resources you need to succeed. However, not all schools comply with this law. If your school is failing you in this area, turn to chapter 9 to learn about activism.

Additionally, students who have trouble at home or who

have other personal issues may need extra help to keep their grades up. For example, if you're hungry, it's hard to focus on a test. If you're depressed, it's hard to get to class. Your school must provide guidance counseling and education plans for students in crisis.

The right to learn in a nondiscriminatory environment.

Discrimination against students based on gender, race, disability, or national origin is illegal in public schools, thanks to Title VII of the Civil Rights Act in our federal law.

The right to wear clothes consistent with your gender identity.

Under federal law, schools can have dress codes, but they cannot force students to wear clothes that don't conform with the student's gender identity.

To go to a bathroom or locker room consistent with your gender identity . . . sometimes.

Not every state protects the rights of transgender people. The Transgender Law Center (transgenderlawcenter.org) has an equality map that tracks each state. Find out if you're protected.

The right to form a club.

If a school allows noncurricular clubs, you are allowed to form an identity-based club, such as a group for Black Girls in Tech, a women's rights group, or a gay-straight alliance. Your school cannot treat it any differently than other noncurricular clubs.

The right to feel safe against harassment and violence.

Title IX, another federal law, protects students against harassment and violence.

The right to have your information kept private.
If you go to a private school, you should read your individual
school policy or ask an administrator about this. Usually
they have to comply with the ADA, but they don't always
have to comply with Title VII or Title IX or protect LGBTQ
students.

If your rights have been violated and the school refuses
to listen to you, contact the American Civil Liberties Union
(ACLU). They should be able to connect you to local legal
resources. If you're the victim of a crime, notify an authority
figure you trust to discuss options. Depending on the nature
of the crime, the authority figure may be obliged to notify
the police.

KNOW THAT STRESS IS MANAGEABLE

School is stressful. There's so much pressure on students to
do well and participate in a million activities. It's not fair to
say things like "Don't get so stressed out!" or "Calm down!"
and "It's not a big deal!" Everyone gets stressed out from
time to time, and saying these things isn't going to make their
homework any easier.

That said, you don't have to suffer emotionally and
physically as a result of stress. Too much stress can cause
burnout, which has awful side effects including lack of sleep,
weight gain or loss, skin problems, depression, weakened
immune system, anxiety, and more. If anything, being
stressed out will *hurt* your scholarly performance—and
possibly your health.

A Difficult Scholarly Bitch knows they have to study,
write papers, and apply for colleges, and that all of this is
extremely challenging. However, they also know that they
don't have to feel overwhelmed in order to feel like they're
being productive. They know that if they feel anxiety or
panic, they should do one of the following:

Meditate.

Meditation requires no special equipment or facilities, and it can be done in sessions as short as a few minutes if you're pressed for time. Even brief meditation sessions can reduce stress. Check chapter 4 for more on this topic.

Exercise.

Take a break and go for a run or do some yoga. Clear your head and soak up the endorphins for twenty minutes. The work will be there when you get back.

Sleep.

Get as much sleep as you can. Teenagers need about nine to nine and a half hours of sleep each night, but they usually only get seven. Sleep deprivation will make your panic much, *much* worse, and make everything feel as if it's high stakes.

Eat well.

Food like sugar and processed carbohydrates will spike your cortisol levels. Cortisol is the hormone responsible for causing stress. Eat well and avoid junk.

Organize.

Stress rises when you feel like things are out of control. So, *take control*. Sit down and make a calendar or list of everything you have on your plate. Make it colorful and fun. Add in breaks. There is also a variety of apps you can download to help manage your schedule or track your time. When you see everything laid out in front of you in an organized way, life won't feel as terrifying.

Don't compare yourself to others or try to win the stress Olympics.

"I'm soooo busy and stressed." "No, *I'm* so busy and

stressed." At first glance, there's nothing wrong with this exchange. On a deeper level, though, neither person is listening to the other, and it's almost a competition. You don't *want* to be busier and more stressed than someone else. That's no fun. Also, maybe your friend just needs someone to listen to them for a sec before they can truly listen to *you*. A Difficult Scholarly Bitch doesn't play the stress Olympics, because she knows nobody wins.

Keep impulsive complaining to a minimum.
We all complain, and it's good to voice complaints if you can make change and stand up for yourself. But sometimes we complain just to make conversation, and we don't even notice that it's painting a negative sheen on our whole day. A Difficult Scholarly Bitch is conscious of complaining too much because she knows that it's more constructive to be positive.

Reduce your workload.
If you organize your work yet you still feel overwhelmed and stressed, maybe you can control the source. Drop an extracurricular activity if it's not serving you anymore. Partner up if you study better with a friend. Occasionally, you might even ask a teacher for a deadline extension, as long as you have a good reason and really need that extra time.

Ask yourself: Is the stress coming from schoolwork or someplace else?
We've been talking about stress from schoolwork, but what about stress from being bullied, from bad social situations, or from problems at home? It's harder to focus on your quiz, for example, if you come to school hungry or if you fear getting tormented by a classmate. It's important to look at all possible causes of stress when you try to manage it.

Ask for help.

Stress has a weird way of making you feel like you're all alone and like you're the only one struggling. It's simply not true. About eight in ten Americans experience stress, and help is out there. If you're suffering, talk to a trusted adult or your school guidance counselor. Let them know that you're feeling very stressed and anxious about school. They might be able to give you stress management techniques or get you the professional help you need.

SCHOOL ISN'T FOREVER

As a bona fide adult, I can promise you that school isn't forever. It's over in the blink of an eye, and you'll wonder what you did with that time. Were you busy obsessing about other peoples' expectations, or your own expectations? Did you put yourself down, or did you love and challenge yourself? Did you stand up to ask for help, or did you hide?

A Difficult Scholarly Bitch wants to fall on the right side of their own history.

BROWSING
WITH WISDOM

Simply put, a Difficult Online Bitch does not engage in internet habits that will harm her or others. This is easier said than done when there's so much opportunity to be a thoughtless asshole online.

The internet is a wonderful and tricky universe. It gives people access to resources around the world. You can learn anything or connect with anybody. Social movements have been birthed on the internet. Marginalized people have found a voice. Everything from education to news to charitable donating has become way more convenient and accessible. A smartphone, a search engine, or a social media platform can connect people in countless ways.

However, the internet is like the Wild West: People can often do whatever they want, and it's hard to control. Every day, people have to deal with the internet's most dangerous aspects, such as cyberbullying, privacy violations, and criminal behavior.

Here are the ground rules for using the internet like a Difficult Bitch:

USE THE INTERNET FOR GOOD

There are a lot of things you *shouldn't* do online, and we'll talk about those. But before the finger wagging begins, let's talk about the good side of the internet.

Here are some ways you probably already use the internet for good:

- **study**
- **research**
- **learn new skills**
- **connect with friends**
- **connect with classmates or teachers in an educational forum**
- **share something important to you**
- **start a conversation**
- **build a website about something you enjoy or care about**
- **raise awareness about a cause**
- **find and participate in supportive communities**
- **organize an event or project**
- **read the news that interests you**
- **follow the work of figures you admire**
- **listen to music or podcasts**
- **build a creative project or portfolio**
- **find style or decor inspiration**
- **find health and fitness tips**
- **handle personal banking**
- **apply for jobs or schools**
- **watch shows or play games (beware of addiction though; see page 96)**

There's so much you can do online that's healthy and safe. A Difficult Online Bitch should stick to these activities.

LET'S GET THIS OUT OF THE WAY: NO NUDES, NO SHADY STRANGERS, NO HATE, NO CRIMES

Anything you do online can bite you in the ass later in life. You don't need anything derailing the Difficult Bitchiness that you've worked so hard to achieve. So here are the most crucial ground rules of internet use:

No nude pictures of yourself or your peers anywhere. Owning your sexuality and loving your body are key aspects of being a Difficult Bitch. There are a lot of healthy, private, safe ways to do that. But if you post or send nude or sexy pics of yourself ANYWHERE, they can easily wind up in the wrong hands and get disseminated all over the internet. If you're a minor and law enforcement sees your photo, they will tell your parents about it and drag your family through a grueling process to see if there's anything nefarious going on, such as child trafficking or family abuse. That will *suck.* So just don't share these types of photos, and tell your friends not to either. It's not worth it. Express yourself differently.

Beware of strangers on the internet.
It's not fair to say, "Don't talk to strangers online" or "Never meet up with someone who you met online." A lot of relationships are forged online, whether through gaming, social media, or online groups with shared interests. If you engage with strangers, watch out for these signs, *especially* while you are still a minor. (Some of these warnings apply to people you know too—most sexual assaults are committed by someone the victim knows.)

- **If a person is pressing you for personal info about where you live, your family, or your school, that's a bad sign. A genuine person who is trying to make a connection doesn't need that information. Do NOT give anyone this information online unless you definitely know them.**

- If they're pressing you for photos or videos of yourself, particularly pornographic ones, block and delete them. Report the interaction to law enforcement immediately if you're a minor.
- If they're pushing you to meet privately and in person out of nowhere, that's weird. For example, maybe you're having a very casual chat with someone through an online fan group, and they suddenly escalate to demanding a one-on-one meeting when that's not even on your radar. Block them.
- If they're making big claims, like that they have celebrity connections or that they can make you an Instagram star, they are definitely lying. Bigwig agencies don't connect with talent that way, and they certainly don't do that with minors. Block.
- If they're contacting you incessantly, they might be trying to overwhelm you so that you don't have the space to think or talk to others. Disengage. Block. Delete.
- If a stranger tells you to download something, don't. It could be malware.
- Watch out for unusual posting history. A liar might not have a lot of photos or information about themselves online, they might not have been posting for very long, or their websites and social media platforms may seem incomplete or strange.

The best thing you can do is block and delete these people immediately and not engage further. You don't know what they're capable of, and you don't need that mess in your life.

HYPOTHETICAL

Mike was excited to go to Comic-Con for the first time. He joined an online group filled with teens who were discussing travel plans and costumes for the upcoming con. He specifically connected with a fellow teenager named Shawn who came from a high school about three hours from his own. They'd been chatting for months about their likes and dislikes in the Marvel and DC universes. When Comic-Con was approaching, Shawn asked Mike if he'd like to meet up in person at the event. Mike said sure. Shawn gave Mike his number and said to stay in touch.

Mike brought his dad to Comic-Con. Mike was too young to travel by himself, and besides, his dad was kind of curious about the hype. Mike texted Shawn, and they agreed to meet at a floor exhibit. Mike and his dad met Shawn, who had brought his older sister and another friend. They all hit it off and spent the rest of Comic-Con together. They kept in touch afterward too.

This is an example of a *good* relationship that can be forged on the internet. Shawn and Mike had developed a real connection online for months before Shawn even brought up an in-person meetup, and the meetup took place at one of the most public events in the world. Shawn gave Mike *his* number and didn't pressure him to reciprocate. Still, you never know, so it's a good thing that Mike went to the meetup with his dad as a buddy. Turns out Shawn was legit, and now he and Mike's friendship is stronger. Let's give it up for Shawn and Mike for being safe and not creepy.

Don't do or discuss anything illegal.
Always assume that your digital activity is being watched, or that it could come up in a court case at some point. This may sound paranoid, but it's actually not that hard to avoid illegal activity online, so you might as well.

Avoid racism, ableism, fatphobia, xenophobia, anti-Semitism, transphobia, sexism, homophobia, or anything you don't actually believe.

If you've made it this far in the book, you probably aren't intentionally racist, ableist, or anything listed above.

However, sometimes people say insensitive stuff to their friends. Maybe you don't usually tell racist jokes, but you happened to hear one that would make your friends laugh because it's so outrageous. Here's a good rule of thumb: if you don't really believe something and it could offend people, keep it off of social media, email, or even texts. You don't have control over these things once they're out in the world, and they are out there forever. You don't want to be characterized by something you said in passing that you don't truly believe.

A NOTE FROM SHARON
SEEING SLURS ONLINE, OR WHY WORDS DO MATTER

Never let anyone tell you that the things that happen on the internet aren't real, or that nothing that goes on there matters. Words on a screen can hurt just as much as words that are spoken to your face. The internet can hurt, and if slurs were grenades, social media can sometimes seem like a minefield, where you can click on any random profile and be exposed to the kind of views that are really ugly and hurtful.

The internet can be a cesspool of some of the vilest, most racist thoughts that most people wouldn't dare say out loud but feel comfortable spouting online because they get to hide behind anonymity. It can be a place for people to vent and share the views that aren't acceptable to share in polite society (for good reason—no one wants to hear racist filth). And sometimes? Those people are friends we thought we could trust.

Here's a scenario many people can probably relate to. A friend of a friend posts on social media a joke that's super racist and gross. You scroll through the comments, expecting to see your friends calling out the friend who posted, but instead, they've liked the post, or even worse, they're laughing about it in the comments.

Ouch. The sudden feeling of betrayal, embarrassment, shame—all of it can hit you like a truck and make you sick to your stomach. But what do you do when your feelings are hurt by something you read or saw online and no one else seems to get it? Should you fight that battle, or let it go? And how can you go on being friendly with your lab partner now that you know they think blackface is funny?

First, assess the situation. Is it worth it? Are you likely to be outnumbered? While I'm not saying that you should bite your tongue, if there are half a dozen people posting in favor of the so-called joke, you should consider if you feel like using your energy to potentially argue online with all those people—especially if they don't seem like they're interested in listening or learning.

In some cases, a major step in the right direction can be to take the conversation offline. If this is someone you care about, then it might be worth an IRL conversation. But if it's your sixth-grade best friend's half brother? Well then, good riddance; you moved out of that town and will never see that guy again anyway.

And if you find yourself encountering things online that hurt you more often than you like? Disconnecting can be hugely beneficial to your mental health. Trust us, you'll definitely live.

LISTEN TO YOURSELF, NOT SOMEONE ELSE

Don't do something online just because someone else is doing it. For example, just because a friend posts salacious pics of themselves on Instagram and says it's okay, that doesn't mean it's a good, safe idea. It just means that they *can* do it. Don't look to your friends or peers for guidance online. Look to yourself, and maybe some wise adults.

DON'T BE IMPULSIVE

This is hard, because you can do *anything* on the internet at any time without thinking about it. You're always being told what to do in school and at home, but on the internet, it's largely up to you to self-regulate. Every time you engage online, ask yourself if you're practicing good judgment or if you could hurt yourself or someone else or get in trouble. Take a deep breath before you hit Send or Post. This might take a lot of self-control, but it's nothing you can't handle.

SHOULDA COULDA WOULDA

Can you think of something you've done online that you regret?

Instead of feeling ashamed about it, dig deep. Why did you post it (or send it or whatever)? What circumstances influenced your choice? Were you feeling angry, or were you prompted by someone else? Break down the situation and analyze your reaction so that the next time you encounter something similar, you won't act as impulsively.

KNOW YOUR INTERNET RIGHTS

Photos you post on social media are not technically considered private. However, if your personal photos or videos are being spread on the internet without your permission, you can legally get them taken down.

If the photos or videos being shared are pornographic in nature, you might be able to press child pornography charges. However, these things take time, a lot of damage is done in the meantime, and the process is a nightmare. Avoid this situation entirely by *only sending or posting photos that you want the whole world to see.*

You also have the right to protect your original material. Nobody can plagiarize your creative work, for example, or repost it without crediting you. Go to copyright.gov to get general information about copyright infringement online.

DISENGAGE FROM MAJOR DRAMA

If you find yourself in the middle of an online fight, gossip exchange, or bullying session, disengage as best as you can. Remember, online words are permanent, and wild stuff happens in the heat of the moment. Stay quiet rather than firing off a response that could escalate things further. Document any abusive or hateful language, and report cyberbullying to an adult.

A NOTE FROM SHARON
A CAUTIONARY TALE

Meet Shelly. Shelly had self-esteem issues from being the only Black girl at a predominantly white school. Shelly grew up feeling ugly because she didn't look like her friends, and the boys and girls at her school seemed to notice everyone else but her.

Then Shelly found a group online dedicated to talking about how beautiful and wonderful Black girls are. Wow, what a change, right? Shelly couldn't believe that such a place existed, and that there were cute boys commenting on pictures of girls like her, saying how much they wished they could date the girl in the picture. Maybe she wouldn't be the only one of her friends without a boyfriend for long, she thought. She began messaging one of the guys she saw commenting often, and he seemed like a dream come true at first. He didn't wish that she looked different—in fact, he was always complimenting her, and he gushed over her skin especially. Only it got to be a little too much. It was all he seemed to talk about. He didn't seem to care about her thoughts or feelings or what she liked to do in her free time. When she did finally meet up with her so-called prince (in a well-lit, public place), it became clear that he didn't really see her as fully human at all, and he was only interested in one thing.

Here's what Shelly needed to know: Be careful and avoid fetishists online. If you're used to seeing hate online toward girls who look like you, it can be almost too easy to gobble up any kind of positive reactions that seem like love and appreciation. An "I love Black girls" Facebook group full of guys you know won't hit you with the "I don't date Black girls" line can seem like a safe, affirming space. But manipulators and predators can wear many different faces. Be careful, and love yourself first so that the perceived love of others won't feel so vital.

KNOW WHEN TO BAIL

A Difficult Online Bitch does not troll, bully, or dox (put someone's private information on the internet). When faced with a conflict online, she asks thoughtful questions and offers openhearted answers. If it's not worth it, she walks away. Perhaps she transfers her thoughts to a forum she finds more meaningful, like a school newspaper or poetry. Unfortunately, when it comes to internet debates, many people aren't looking to learn; they're looking to win. This can lead to circular, endless arguments, not to mention a ton of wasted time and frustration on your part. And for what, so you can convert your friend's step-uncle to your point of view? Who cares?

It's so easy to just shout at a wall on the internet when you're feeling upset or offended—especially when you're not using your real or full name. But a Difficult Online Bitch doesn't have anything to hide. She does everything online with purpose and forethought. She also knows she can make a much bigger difference if she channels her energy elsewhere.

DISCONNECT

This is the hardest thing for some people to do. From time to time, take a daylong break from your phone. Delete a social media app that doesn't serve you very much. Let it go. Put your texts on Do Not Disturb for a week during the hours you need to sleep or focus. Go on a supersafe hike with friends and turn off all your phones. No checking texts, no selfies, no posting. Let it just be an experience you share in real life.

Try these things out and see if you're still alive and thriving. Chances are, you will be.

It's important to take healthy breaks from your phone so you can stay present, connect with people, and remind yourself that the internet isn't really *that* important in the scope of your real life. You may also realize how much you use your phone when you *can't* use it anymore. A Difficult Online Bitch can resist the temptation to keep scrolling.

ACKNOWLEDGE ADDICTION

The internet can act on our dopamine receptors. You've probably experienced a little rush when someone likes your posts on social media. That's dopamine, a chemical in our brains, and even Difficult Online Bitches love dopamine. Everyone does.

However, some people get addicted to the internet as a result of the dopamine rushes. Sometimes you can't even tell you're addicted because checking your phone all day every day is so normalized. If you're concerned, you can track your usage and assess yourself. Your phone should have a basic application for this, or you can download apps that tell you how much time you spend checking your phone, emails, text, and social media. Some apps can help you curb your usage and become more mindful about it.

It's possible for someone to get so addicted to things like online games, porn, gambling, shopping, or social media "likes" that it doesn't look much different from a narcotic addiction. They might be online all day, disengaged from real relationships or activities, not taking care of themselves physically, or spending way more money than they used to. Usually, they're not actually having fun. Internet addiction is a very serious illness that ruins lives. Thankfully, there is treatment out there. If you need help with an internet addiction—or if you know someone who does—a good place to start would be the Substance Abuse and Mental Health Services Administration national helpline at 1-800-662-HELP.

CHAPTER 7

THE DIFFICULT
EXTRACURRICULAR BITCH

PUSHING YOURSELF

School takes up a lot of your life, and most students are encouraged to also participate in extracurricular activities such as sports, clubs, student government, plays, debate teams, exchange programs, or volunteer groups. Hopefully you choose to participate in certain activities that you love.

You've probably been told that you need extracurriculars to get into college, and that's absolutely true. A Difficult Extracurricular Bitch knows about these requirements and understands that she's accountable for her future, whether she's going to college, taking a few years off, or pursuing some other fulfilling alternative.

What makes her difficult is that she brings her own fire to her extracurricular life. She embraces curiosity. She pushes herself. She thinks outside the box. Maybe she even leads. But she also knows when to chill out.

DO SOMETHING YOU LOVE

Extracurriculars provide the opportunity to explore your talents and interests. If you're having trouble choosing which to participate in, start by thinking about what you love, and go from there. For just a minute, don't worry about what your friends are doing, especially if they don't share your interests. Whether you're into music, dance, art, math, activism, volunteering, or sports, there may be something perfect for you in your school or larger community. Don't wait for the info to come to you. A Difficult Extracurricular Bitch has to be proactive by asking around and doing her research.

DO SOMETHING THAT SCARES YOU A LITTLE

It's easy to close doors and say, "I can't." But a Difficult Extracurricular Bitch is brave. She'll try rock climbing or mentoring, even if it makes her a little nervous, because she's not afraid to fail. You never know whether you can do something until you've tried—and more often than not, your capabilities will surprise you.

IT'S NOT A LIFE SENTENCE

There's a good chance that you won't do your extracurriculars as a job. You may not even do them in college, unless you're planning to get a scholarship based on one of them. What you do in high school—and beyond—isn't a life sentence. You can reinvent yourself a thousand times from now until you're 105 years old. Don't worry about getting "locked in" to something, even if you excel at it and everyone around you is telling you to pursue it as a career. If you're in the National Economics Challenge and it's fulfilling for you, that doesn't mean you're signing a contract to be an economist when you grow up. See it instead as a fun opportunity to try something new or explore a passion, no strings attached.

DON'T LET A BAD ORGANIZATION RUIN YOUR DRIVE

Sometimes, an extracurricular seems absolutely perfect, but it turns out to suck. Usually this is because a club or activity is neglected for some reason. There might be bad leadership, no funds, disorganization, a lack of passion, a decrepit meeting space—you name it. An organization is only as good as the sum of its parts. The film club in your school might boast only two members with a janky projector. But that film club could be a thriving place if it had funds to buy better equipment, enthusiastic and organized leadership, a clear sense of purpose, and promotion that drew in more members.

You don't have to settle for crappy extracurriculars. If you're really passionate about, say, film club, you can help get the club on track. It's not like Algebra II, where you have no power to stop your teacher from talking about asymptotes. Extracurriculars, especially student-run ones, are easier to change. You can start by talking to club members about what they want, by talking to administrators about what can be done to improve the situation, and by promoting the club around school once it's up and running.

BE A LEADER

Leadership means stepping up to make decisions, supporting your peers, and getting your voice heard. You can be a student government representative, a team captain, an editor of a school newspaper, president of the robotics club—the opportunities are endless. A Difficult Extracurricular Bitch knows that she needs to earn these positions, however. She leads by example and due process, and she knows that these positions mean more work and responsibility—not just a fun title.

You don't need to rush to take charge. A good leader learns first by listening and observing.

A leader doesn't even need to have a title like president or chair. Some people can lead one-on-one with someone who needs mentoring. Or they lead the design vision for the team logo, but not the whole operation. Behind-the-scenes leaders make the world go round.

Finally, remember that students have the right to form clubs. Check with your school policy for any guidelines, but generally you should be able to start anything from an identity-based meetup to alternative athletics. If you go to public school, the administration must treat your club equally to other student-initiated clubs. All clubs and extracurriculars fall under Titles VII and IX, which means that schools are responsible for ensuring that clubs and athletics are free of discrimination and harassment.

LOOK OUTSIDE OF SCHOOL

Depending on where you live, you may be able to find extracurriculars in your area outside of school. You can volunteer at the library, assistant coach for Little League, audition for community theater, or look into adventure or travel programs. Make sure to do a little research beforehand, and only work with vetted, reputable organizations.

IF YOU'RE SICK OF IT, PRACTICE POSITIVE THINKING

It's easy to fall into a daily grind mindset and think, "Ugh, this is a slog." It's hard to feel lucky when you're working so hard and when you're expected to put nearly as much time into extracurriculars as you put into school.

Here's where a Difficult Extracurricular Bitch can add perspective. Sure, she's busy and taxed, and it's hard to get to soccer practice all the time, plus there's that one dude in Key Club who annoys the bejesus out of her. But here's a boring dose of reality: Grown-ups rarely make the time to do activities like these. Even if they love soccer, they rarely join teams or fun clubs. They rarely even learn new skills. It's not because they have no interests. It's because there's no time, priorities change, and things like clubs and education are way less accessible for adults. Yes, this *will* happen to you someday to some extent, and you'll remember high school extracurriculars as something you loved, something you hated, or something you wasted by taking them for granted and complaining about them.

Thinking positively takes practice, just like soccer.

It means letting negative thoughts slide and reminding yourself of the upsides: "I'm curious to see where this takes me," and "Here's what I love about soccer practice even though it's challenging." Remember why you chose the activity and what you like about it. It will make the work more fun, and the fact that these activities help you get into college is just a bonus.

SHOULDA COULDA WOULDA

Have you ever quit something or walked away from something—and then regretted it later?

Maybe it happened in a fit of emotion during a difficult moment. Or maybe the activity scared you. What were you feeling? What was happening when you felt that way?

The next time you feel scared or emotional during an activity, consider taking a break and giving yourself some time to mull it over before quitting completely.

IF YOU'RE STILL SICK OF IT, MAYBE YOU NEED A CHANGE

Sometimes you've put in your best effort, but you just don't want to do an activity anymore. Maybe your time is better spent on a different activity. Maybe you're overextended and need a break. Maybe you've tried to get along with the group, and it's not working out. Maybe you're going through something personal that you need to work on with a counselor or on your own. If you're having a frustrating time because of one specific incident or one particularly difficult encounter, you might want to wait until the dust settles before you decide to quit.

However, if the activity isn't serving your life, make a change.

HYPOTHETICAL

This is a true story about me again.

I come from a very sports-heavy family. I played Little League, so it only seemed natural for me to play high school softball and tennis. These activities took up all of my extracurricular time. I was starting to realize that I was actually pretty mediocre at those sports, and I was culture-shocked by the newly intense, competitive pressure. Nobody had cared so much in Little League!

Still, for about a year and a half, I stayed in these sports because I didn't know any different. I kept thinking that if I just played enough, I would find the hidden burning passion inside of me. I hadn't asked myself, "Why am I doing this?"

Here's the thing, though: I was always a theater performer at heart. I had this amazing voice that I'd inherited from my grandma, and I loved the energy and attention that the theater provided. Acting came naturally to me. I loved making people laugh. So, against all of my prior conditioning, I dipped my toe into the theater world— just to check it out at first. It was scary. I was a jock. My jock friends poked fun at me a little. Plus, the theater club already had its own social hierarchy, and everyone was wary of the new jock in town.

But over time, I landed awesome roles and made lasting theater friends. (I even got them to hang out with my jock friends sometimes!) I also *didn't* get a lot of lead roles. I fell on my face and failed too. I had a lot to learn from the more professionally trained students.

Slowly but surely, I abandoned sports entirely and moved to theater full-time. Why fight it?

It was hard to tell my family that I was quitting sports. I danced around it and minimized it. I expected them to be crushed. And in some families, that might have been the case.

But luckily for me, my family completely understood and encouraged the change. It must have been clear to them that my sports career had plateaued, and that my true passion and talents were in the theater.

And even if they *had* tried to stop me, I was mature enough to make my own choices.

There's no freer feeling than realizing you've been stuck, owning it, and taking action to change. That's true growth. Switching to theater was one of my first major Difficult Bitch decisions, which is why I still haven't forgotten it decades later.

AVOID OVERLOAD

Just like school, extracurriculars can get intense and stress you out. There are highs and lows, successes and failures. Sometimes you'll need help getting motivated, while other times you might feel overwhelmed.

But if you're feeling totally overwhelmed *all the time*, ease up on yourself and reset your priorities. Be realistic. You might *want* to become president of the aeronautics club and also take the lacrosse team to nationals while volunteering at a soup kitchen on weekends, but you really probably don't have time for it all.

In the end, choose what fills your soul. Only put in what you can. Practice mindfulness (go to chapter 4 for more on that) and lean on your support system. You shouldn't have to feel like shit all the time when these things are supposed to be fun and fulfilling. You literally don't have to do any of the things in this chapter if you've tried them out and they're not for you. A Difficult Extracurricular Bitch can absorb advice, take it when it's helpful, and drop it if it's making her miserable.

You might be a very serious student who says this lax attitude is impossible. Maybe you're the star of the track team and the pressure on you is unrelenting and there's no way out. Maybe your parents have instilled in you that becoming president of your regional debate team is hands-down the most important thing in the world. Everyone has different values when it comes to extracurricular activities. Just remember that you are getting old enough to choose your own path, and if your chosen path includes a lot of pressure, then you *must* exercise tons of self-care. If you just keep going and going without checking in on yourself, you'll burn out and resent the world. See pages 79–82 for self-care tactics in the face of burnout.

A NOTE FROM ZARA
SHOW THEM WHAT YOU'RE MADE OF

If you had asked me about the importance of extracurriculars when I was in high school, I would have told you that they're an absolute *must*. "Everyone has to do lots of extracurriculars! They help you *find yourself*, and without them high school is meaningless!" is along the lines of what I would have said. And I would have done so in extremely dramatic fashion, because like Halley, I was a total theater kid.

But as an adult, I understand that not everyone has the sort of access to extracurriculars that I enjoyed. I had parents who could afford to enroll me in lots of activities and a mom who drove me to each one. I had the carefree attitude of a kid who didn't have to get a job in order to afford things like clothes or food. I was really, really lucky.

That privilege gave me the opportunity to explore lots of extracurriculars before honing in on what I really loved. I know there are kids out there who don't have a parent at home to take them to extracurriculars. I know there are kids who can't afford ballet classes or can't buy a baseball glove. I know there are kids who are too busy working, helping raise siblings, or taking on at-home responsibilities.

If you're lucky enough to have access to extracurricular activities, I hope you'll decide to take advantage of that. And I hope you'll keep an open mind, follow your passions, and chart your own path.

Let's be real for a second: That whole "do what you love!" adage is easier for some people than it is for others. Maybe you dream of playing a sport, but your disability makes it impossible for you to do so on your school's team. Maybe you long to start a band, but your parents come from a culture that views your favorite music as a waste of time. Maybe you want to join an athletics team, but you're gay and worry about hazing. Or maybe you'd crush it on the football team, but you're not allowed to join because you're a girl. Whatever the case may be, the proverbial playing field isn't always equal—but as a Difficult Bitch, you have it in you to fight for your right to try the things that interest you. And we hope you'll break down the barriers that stand between you and your passions.

As the child of Asian immigrants, I didn't see a lot of people in my community who were into the arts, but I decided to throw myself into them anyway. It wasn't always easy. I didn't see anyone who looked like me on TV shows, in movies, or in the Broadway community— and I won't lie, a part of me felt like the performing arts industry was closed off to people like me. I had to defy stereotypes (turns out sometimes the brown kid is bad at math and good at singing!), but in the end, it was worth it. Being involved in theater didn't feed me into a career or earn me a scholarship, but it *did* give me something to love. It helped me shed some of my shyness, make some unexpected friends, and dream big.

In part, my doing extracurriculars is why I now understand that not everyone has the privileges I had. When you step out of your comfort zone and try new things, you meet people you may not typically cross paths with, and you can learn so much. That's the value of extracurriculars: they open you up in the most wonderful way, and that can shape your perspective for life.

So do something bold and unexpected. Play an instrument even if your friends think it's nerdy. Try out for a sports team even if you don't fit the mold of what a typical player looks like. Do things you're not particularly good at, do things you excel at—if you're lucky enough to have the resources and time, *do as many things as you can*. Because extracurriculars aren't just things that may get you into college (even though that sure doesn't hurt!). They're also the things that may make you *you*.

A NOTE ON PRIVILEGE

This whole chapter assumes that you have time to do extracurricular, non-job activities. It assumes that you or your parents have the money to pay for things like equipment and supplies, club dues, or travel expenses. It assumes you're able to get transportation to and from these things on a regular basis, and that you'll live in the same town long enough to remain involved in the same activities. So many circumstances beyond your control might make it difficult or impossible for you to participate in extracurricular activities. Because you're a Difficult Empowered Bitch, you should be pissed off at me for making these assumptions.

Yes, there are ways to get exemptions on payments if you talk to the athletics director. There are scholarships and nonprofits that raise money to help kids who don't have enough funds to participate. You can carpool. If you move a lot, you can look into organizations with wider networks, like Kiwanis Club or state-run intramural sports programs.

There are ways. We already know that a Difficult Extracurricular Bitch is resourceful. But I'm not going to lie to you and tell you that the world is a fair place. People with less privilege have to work much, much harder to get what they deserve than people who have plenty of privilege. Most Difficult Bitches in history have recognized this, and they've fought against it. To join the fight, check out chapter 9.

KNOWING YOUR WORTH

A Difficult Bitch balances her finances in a smart way.

Our culture is so obsessed with money that you certainly don't need me to tell you it matters. Maybe you already babysit or get allowances or have part-time jobs. Maybe you're already worrying about how you'll afford college or rent after high school. The goal of this chapter is not to make you even more nervous about money. On the other hand, if you never think about money now, that'll backfire when you have to deal with it on a grander scale.

For now, a Difficult Financial Bitch should aim for a basic understanding of personal finance principles. It's unlikely that he'll become financially independent in high school, so he should use this time to learn some essentials that will be helpful down the road.

WHAT'S YOUR RELATIONSHIP WITH MONEY?

Everyone has a different relationship with money, usually depending on how they grew up. Some families are very anxious about spending money. Others have never had money, so they sometimes resent people who have it, but they may also harbor dreams of making millions one day. In some families, nobody ever, ever talks about money, which makes it a scary mysterious thing. Other families *only* talk about money, which makes it the most important measure of success and happiness.

As you start to become more independent, your relationship with money will shift around, but you'll always have those family values branded into your brain somewhere.

At its core, though, finance is just about numbers. The more you save, the more you have. The more educated you are, the more prepared you will be. A Difficult Bitch faces finances head-on so that she can be responsible and meet her financial goals (within reason).

A NOTE FROM SHARON
ACCESS YOUR RESOURCES.

What can you do when there's no one to teach you the ins and outs of being financially responsible (because your parents are still putting the occasional bill in your name)? Fortunately, there are all types of resources out there for people looking to educate themselves on being financially healthy. The internet is full of information, but there are plenty of IRL options too. Check out your local library for basic (and free) classes, and look online for financial groups (on topics like investing and building generational wealth) that meet in person and are specifically created for young Black people.

SHOULDA COULDA WOULDA

Have you ever noticed that you think very differently about money than your friends do?

Maybe you don't think about money that much, but you have a friend who never wants to do activities that require money. Or maybe you're a bit frugal, but you have a friend or relative who spends money like it's nothing.

There's no "right" way here. But it's important to observe yourself and other people so you can be an empathetic Difficult Financial Bitch—and also so you can see there are other ways to think about money. Nobody holds the absolute truth.

PERSONAL FINANCE 101

Let's go over some basics. No matter what circumstances you were born into, these things will apply to you at some point in your life.

Financial Goals

Setting financial goals is an important exercise. For example, maybe you'd like to own a car in five years. Maybe you'd like to hit $500 in a savings account in one year. Everyone's goals look a little different. And remember: Plans change. You might decide that your goal wasn't reasonable, or that you'd rather spend money on something else.

Income

Your income is the money you have. It's your wages from work, plus your allowance or that birthday money from your aunt. Most people have little to no income in high school, and they depend on their caregivers. It usually takes many years beyond high school to build an independent income.

Expenses

Once you live on your own, you have expenses that you need to pay regularly. For example, you might have to pay monthly rent on your apartment or car payments or a streaming service subscription. Ideally, your income is higher than your expenses so that you can afford your basic expenses and still have money to spare.

Loan

When you borrow money—be it from a relative, a credit card company, or a bank—it's called a loan. Usually, you have to pay it back with interest, which means that you promise to pay back extra in order to borrow the money. Interest rates vary depending on the loan.

Checking Account

If you're fourteen or older, you can open a checking account with a parent or guardian. Once you're eighteen, you can get an account on your own. If you have cash, you put it in your checking account. If you want to spend cash, you take it from your checking account. A *debit card* allows you to make purchases with the money that's in your checking account. It is a fast way to access this cash. You can also write checks or get this cash from an ATM.

Credit Card

You can get a credit card through a bank at the age of eighteen. People usually apply for credit cards around the time they start earning a steady income. Every time you use a credit card, think of it as taking out a little loan from the bank. A checking account contains your money that you earned or received. A credit card is not your money. You have to pay it back every month with whatever is in your checking account. If you don't, your bank will start charging you for the loan, PLUS interest, which is often lots of extra money tacked on. Banks love it when you have to pay them interest.

So why use a credit card? *If* you make enough money to stay ahead of your bills, it's nice to have that extra loan, and to have a whole month to pay it off.

You also need a credit score to take out big bank loans or to buy houses or cars. If you don't use a credit card at all, your score will be terrible, making it more difficult to procure these things from reputable places.

Also, some credit cards come with cool rewards like travel points or discounts at stores. Debit cards don't usually have anything extra or fun attached.

Debt

Debt is when you owe someone or something money. For example, maybe one month you spend more money on your credit card than you have in your bank account. Now you'll be in debt to the credit card issuer until you have enough money to pay off the bill.

The longer you wait to pay off a loan or a debt, the larger the interest rates and late fees become. Credit card debt, student loan debt, and car loan debt are common.

Consumer debt is up to $13.1 trillion in the US. The high costs of tuition, real estate, and living in general have created a widespread crisis with few good solutions.

A Difficult Financial Bitch is not immune to the economy, but he'll stay informed and do his best to keep his debt manageable. He'll also join the political fight to demand fairer debt practices.

Student Loans

College and graduate students often have to borrow money from a bank or the government to pay for tuition and other expenses. Sometimes, they wind up in student debt for decades. Scholarships and financial aid can sometimes help lessen the costs. If your family has the means, they can also invest in a 529, which is a government investment account that helps pay for tuition.

Savings

Savings refers to money that is put away for later. There are many different types of savings accounts, but the most common and simple one is a money market account. You can put money in or take it out anytime. This time, you *want* an account with high interest, because YOU get paid the interest, so you make a little profit from the account. The more you put into it, the more you'll get out of it.

There's no harm in opening up a savings account and contributing to it when you can. (You need a checking account to steer it directly.) Eventually you may have enough to buy a car!

Investment and Trade

Investing in something means you put money into a financial market, a business, or a brand. If that market, business, or brand grows, you earn *more* money back later. If the market or business investment crashes, however, you lose that money. That's the risk of investment.

In personal finance, investment often refers to the money that your bank account is investing for you. For example, in a savings account, the bank is investing your money into different markets and aiming to make you a profit. It's pretty low-risk, and a savings account usually won't turn out a *huge* payout. This is why some people learn the ins and outs of markets and make their own investments.

Trade is a type of investment in which you buy and sell stocks for a profit. A successful trader needs expertise before diving in and potentially losing everything.

A Difficult Financial Bitch will always be smart and educated when it comes to investment.

Get Organized.

For now, a simple rule of thumb is to add up all your monthly expenses (for example, your phone bill, nights out with friends, or books). Put that number into one column. Put your monthly income or allowance into another column. Make sure the expenses column does not add up to more than the income column. Put three-fourths of what's left into a savings account.

However, keep in mind that it might take a while to get to a financial place where you can save, which is completely normal for people just starting out. And remember that you can always take money out of savings and put it into your checking account if needed.

A Difficult Financial Bitch sets goals and does what she can to reach them.

INTERNSHIPS

A Difficult Financial Bitch knows that internships can be great ways to get started in their career early. Interns are temporary employees who are mostly at a business to learn and make connections. Many industries use interns, including publishing, finance, and tech. You can find internships through company websites, online databases, job boards, and school career fairs.

Interns are entitled to minimum wage pay, and they must be able to get something educational or career-growing from the experience. Unless you want to be a barista, you shouldn't be forced to spend your whole time at an internship fetching coffee. Also, a company is not supposed to *need* an intern to function. This rule effectively stops employers from exploiting you for more work than they're paying for. You can report violations of these rules to the US Department of Labor.

A Difficult Financial Bitch will get everything they can out of an internship, including new skills and future networking contacts. If you'd like to branch out into a new department or skill within the company, let your manager know. Their job is to help you grow from the experience, not to stick you in a corner.

GET PAID FROM A JOB

To make a bit of your own money, you can get an after-school job. Look for a place that hires teenagers and will cater to your school hours. Legally, companies can't hire you unless you're at least fourteen, and most jobs require you to be at least sixteen. Common jobs for teens include scooping ice cream, retail, yard work, coaching or refereeing, and babysitting. If you love films, you might get lucky and snag an usher job at your local movie theater. If you're interested in carpentry, maybe you can find a woodshop apprenticeship through your friend's uncle. It doesn't hurt to ask. In the summer, you can spread your wings and try jobs like lifeguarding or camp counseling.

You're probably not going to get rich from these jobs, and most of them are not stepping-stones to a career. And that might be fine for now.

However, if you're skilled at something that people really need, you might be able to make *more* money. Adults in your life might need a coder or a web designer or a knit sweater. Their kids may need a tutor. These adults should pay you for your time.

NEGOTIATE

You probably have to negotiate with your family to get what you want. With jobs, you negotiate for better pay, a promotion, paid time off, and more. A Difficult Financial Bitch must learn how to advocate for herself. Quick tips:

Log your accomplishments.
Before you negotiate with the big boss, make a record of all your accomplishments on the job. Have you been on

time every day? Do customers love you? Write these things down and bring them into the negotiation. If you have *no* accomplishments, or if you're just starting out in the working world, you might want to wait awhile before you try to negotiate.

Do research.

You want to ask for what you're worth, but you don't want to ask for something outrageous, such as seventy-five dollars an hour for a gig at a fast-food restaurant. Your boss will never be able to give that to you, and it will make you seem pretty unreasonable. Look up what other people make in your job. Ask your colleagues. Aim high, but not outrageously high. Ask about raises when you're starting. Some companies have built-in raises every year. You can also ask for a raise anytime you take on significantly more responsibility, as long as you're not asking for raises constantly. Limit it to a couple of times a year.

A NOTE FROM SHARON
ON NEGOTIATING

Sure, it's easy to suggest standing up for yourself and demanding what you're worth, but how do you do that when you already feel like there's a big red arrow pointed at you, singling you out as the one person who doesn't necessarily fit in? If you're preparing yourself to negotiate for a raise or promotion or anything else, it can be tempting to bite your tongue in order to not seem like the so-called angry Black woman. But part of knowing your worth is standing up for what you know you deserve, despite your fears that other people will find flimsy reasons to discount what you're saying.

Remember this: No, you shouldn't just be grateful to be there because you broke the glass ceiling or what-have-you and became the first ever Black woman to land a position at whatever fancy start-up. And no, you shouldn't be quiet and work twice as hard as everyone else just to prove that you aren't a diversity hire who doesn't actually have the skills for the job.

No one is going to stand up for yourself but you. Like Halley said, come armed with your greatest weapons: research and confidence. Do your research and know that what you're asking for is reasonable. Prepare your arguments. Sit up straight and speak clearly. You deserve to be where you are, and you're going to continue to kick ass and fight your way into where you want to be. Leave the doubts at the door. You've got this.

Also leave the anxiety about stereotypes at home—worrying about them doesn't serve you—and hope that whoever you're dealing with does the same. And if they don't? Chances are, there will be a less toxic workplace in your future.

Don't start with an apology.
"I'm so sorry to bring this up, but . . ." "I'm sorry to bother you, but . . ." You have the right to assert yourself and ask for a raise. You're not being a burden. Approach with confidence.

A NOTE FROM SHARON
STOP APOLOGIZING FOR EXISTING.

This is a vital lesson to learn as a Black woman in the workplace. You deserve to occupy whatever space you're in. No, you didn't steal whatever spot from someone more deserving. If you worked your butt off to get to where you are, why doubt yourself? You will encounter people who try to tear you down, but allowing them to occupy your mind takes away attention that you could be devoting to your plans of world domination.

Some a-hole at lunch made a snarky comment about affirmative action loud enough so that you'd hear it? Sounds like a personal problem for them. Let them be angry or resentful or jealous or hateful, and keep on doing you. You are not an imposter.

Ditch the ultimatums and be enthusiastic.

If you come into a negotiation with guns blazing, yelling, "Give me a promotion or I'm quitting!" chances are, your boss will say no. If you angrily demand a raise or whine about your situation, you'll send the message that you hate the job and will probably either quit anyway or be unsatisfied forever. Bosses want to invest in people who are a positive part of the team. You want to show her that you're enthusiastic about the job, that you *want* to stay, and that a raise or promotion would make that more likely.

A "no" today doesn't mean "no" forever.

If your boss says no today, don't take it hard. Get more information. Are they saying no because they don't have the funds? Unless the company is really failing, this *might* just be an excuse. A boss should be able to find a way to pay you at least a *little* more so you'll stay at the job. If not, it may mean they don't value you.

Are they saying no because they don't think you are ready to move up yet? If so, ask your boss to outline what you need to do to get there, and then negotiate again later.

HYPOTHETICAL

Hazel had been working in a local baby clothing store for two summers. She made twelve dollars an hour. She sometimes worked an extra hour without demanding pay because she felt bad for the owner, Sally. Hazel was always on time, and she always had a smile on her face. She liked the work, but she felt she deserved at least fourteen dollars an hour, and she didn't want to work an extra hour for free anymore.

Hazel wrote an email to Sally on a Friday evening saying, "Sally, I'm sick and tired of working an extra hour for free. I need you to track my hours more carefully. Also, I *definitely* should get $14 an hour now. I've been with you forever. Can we start with $14 next week? Cool, thanks."

Sally didn't usually check her email on the weekends. So she didn't open Hazel's message until Monday morning when they were both at work. Hazel was right next to her as she read it, which was awkward for both of them. Sally felt confused and upset. She'd thought Hazel was happy at the store. Hazel was right about being a great employee, and Sally felt terrible that Hazel had been working an extra hour for free—she hadn't noticed. But the tone of this email made Hazel seem like a totally different person. Did she have a secret explosive side? Did she hate the work? Sally didn't respond to the email for the rest of the day, and she even considered firing Hazel for acting so entitled.

Hazel made a lot of mistakes. She wrote an email when she should have talked to Sally in person. Hazel was angry and demanding in the email, which was off-putting to Sally and damaging to their good relationship. Hazel deserves to get a raise and to be paid for her work, but her approach might have killed her chances. Stay professional and enthusiastic, and *don't ask for a raise in an email or text.*

SO YOU WANT TO START A BUSINESS ...

Everyone is an influencer or an entrepreneur these days. Some whiz kids are launching businesses in high school, usually with the help of adults.

Some examples:

- **Forming a cooperative of teen dog walkers or babysitters in your town**
- **Selling a line of crafts on a site like Etsy or at a local market**
- **Designing a game app**
- **Writing or editing an online publication for teens like you**

These ventures usually require money up front to cover the costs of getting started, such as equipment, materials, or a website domain name. So you may need a boost from investors or extremely generous relatives. And once you've got things up and running, you'll need to devote a lot of ongoing work and maintenance to your business to keep it going.

A NOTE FROM SHARON
GETTING A LOAN AS A WOMAN OF COLOR

Is it impossible? No. Will it be harder? Mayybeee.
You probably don't need anyone to tell you this, but discrimination is still a very real thing. What's even worse is that you may not even be able to tell for certain if you're being discriminated against.

Luckily, there are organizations that are committed to trying to level the playing field more. For a little bit of inspiration and to get a feel for what's out there, do a search for "business grants for Black women entrepreneurs." If you're a minority and you're interested in starting a small business, there are a ton of grants that you can apply for. There's also a community that you can access; minority business owners have professional groups where they can connect, and hey, maybe if you check out a meeting, you'll meet someone who can give you the inside scoop on banks that are actually diverse.

Discrimination be damned, Black women are out here killing it in the business world. Statistically speaking, women of color are starting more businesses than any other group, so get your side hustle on, sis!

FIGHT FOR WHAT'S RIGHT

A Difficult Activist Bitch channels her emotions into action. She knows that we can't sit around bickering anymore. Her future is on the line.

The world is very, very, *very* far from perfect. You're probably getting bombarded by depressing news about climate change, school shootings, corporate greed, racism, cancer, immigrant detention, sexism, and everything in between. Perhaps you are experiencing some of these things firsthand. You *should* be angry. You *should* be upset. But most of all, you should be an activist.

Not everyone can be Greta Thunberg or Emma González, the superstar teens who spoke up to the United Nations and the US Congress, respectively. However, anyone can work to effect positive change.

KNOW WHAT WORKS AND WHAT DOESN'T

"Slacktivism" refers to lazy activism, like commenting on articles online or sharing posts on social media. It's not negative, and people *do* get a lot of information from social media. However, it's simply not enough for a world in crisis. In addition, a Difficult Activist Bitch can aim to do one or more of the following actions twice a year:

- Call your local, state, and national representatives and urge them to take action on important issues.
- Volunteer for a political campaign or organization that you believe in.
- Be inclusive in activities you organize at school, in your extracurriculars, and in your personal life.
- Educate yourself and others about sustainability or any activism subject that interests you.
- Participate in protests, cleanups, or fundraisers for activist organizations.
- Write articles for your school paper or letters to the editor of your local paper.
- Volunteer your time and skills toward a nonprofit you care about.
- Create art, media, or a website that contributes to the conversation.

Avoid these actions, which do *not* effect positive change:

- Arguing with random people online (see chapter 6)
- Spreading hate or engaging in violence
- Complaining constantly to friends about the state of the world
- Being a spectator and not a participant
- Excluding people based on gender, race, etc. Anyone can be an ally.

GET EDUCATED

You don't need to be an expert on climate science to participate in a school walkout, or an expert on immigration law to be furious about detention conditions at the border. However, if you're going to throw yourself into a cause, you'll do *much* better work if you educate yourself. You're probably getting a lot of information from your family, friends, and maybe your teachers. A Difficult

Activist Bitch gathers the facts on her own and makes up her own mind.

For example, if you're upset about microplastics in our oceans, look up the history of plastics and see how we got to where we are. Check out what experts are doing to fight it. Get to know the impact of individual plastic use, as well as the basics of corporate and government policies. This will help you figure out where your time and energy are needed most. Plus, you can school the people who disagree with you, which is always fun.

RESPECT NUANCE AND EXPERTISE

Guaranteed: Every issue is more complicated than it seems. You don't know everything, and that's okay. A Difficult Activist Bitch respects that issues are complicated and that some people know a lot more than her. This also motivates her to keep learning. Don't be like online trolls! Aim to learn, not to be right.

CAUSES CAN BE GLOBAL AND LOCAL

Think about causes that interest you. Climate change is a huge issue, for example, and there are endless ways to fight it. On a global level, you can participate in national marches, organize letter-writing campaigns to the US Congress or the United Nations, or raise money for global organizations like the Environmental Defense Fund or the Natural Resources Defense Council.

However, you can also fight on a local level, which might not sound as epic but might actually have more immediate impact. For example, if there's a factory in your town that's polluting the water, you could speak up in town hall or city hall about the polluter, participate in protests, draft a petition for townspeople to sign, and write your concerns to your mayor or district leader. Local nonprofit organizations may be able to help you gather scientific information and more people's support. The chances of toppling that polluter are much greater than your odds of cleaning up the entire planet single-handedly, and you'll get to work on the front lines. However, all levels of activism are valid. Do what you have the time to do well.

IT'S NOT ABOUT THE GLORY

A great deal of activism is boring, to be honest. You might sign up to volunteer for the coolest nonprofit ever, only to find yourself stuffing envelopes.

But frankly, if you're in it for the glory, you are probably doing it for the wrong reasons. Every step matters. Every movement is built on hard work that is often tedious.

That said, if you *really* hate stuffing envelopes, there are many other options. If animal rights are your thing, you can volunteer at a shelter. We tend to think of activism as being very loud and in the streets, but sometimes it's sweeping the floors and walking dogs. You're still an animal rights activist.

HYPOTHETICAL

Alex was excited to start volunteering at the local LGBTQ youth center after school. She heard about an open student volunteer office position there, and she signed up immediately. She had been studying gay political history in class, and in her spare time, she'd read personal essays by LGBTQ youth. She had tons of ideas about how to change laws to be more transgender-friendly.

For now, Alex figured that, as a relatively privileged trans girl with supportive parents, she could help youth who did not have that affirmation in their lives. She could tell them about their rights, give them hugs, and offer them resources and places to stay in town.

When she arrived at the youth center, she found a few young people filling out paperwork in the waiting area. A receptionist sent Alex to a back office to wait for her supervisor, Puja. When Puja finally arrived thirty minutes late, she seemed surprised to see Alex there.

"Ohhh, right—you're the kid who wants to be a lawyer, right?" said Puja. "Welcome."

Alex was told to wait for a while longer while Puja got settled. Alex waited and waited. She watched as a youth walked into Puja's office, closed the door, then exited with some paperwork, wiping tears from her eyes. Alex feared that Puja had forgotten she was there, so she decided to take some initiative.

"Hey, Puja, do you mind if I helped you with the next person who comes in?" said Alex.

"What do you mean?" Puja asked.

"I'm really interested in this type of work, and I'd love to help the youth that come in," said Alex.

Puja smiled. "That's really awesome, but I'm a certified social worker and my sessions with the youth are completely confidential. I can't have you interacting with the youth while you're here—it's against policy—but I was hoping you'd take a look at our social media and website metrics and come up with some ideas to boost our web presence."

Alex was crushed.

So many people have been through this kind of volunteering story. You go into an activism situation hoping for one thing, and what you get is a lukewarm welcome and a disappointing task. Sometimes you get lucky and find an energized organization that embraces you and gives you the work you want, but the opposite happens *all the time*. Puja is probably busy and distracted, and maybe a bit disorganized with her calendar. Now, Alex is basically doing an unpaid job she never wanted. For someone who's into web design and social media, this would be a dream come true. But Alex isn't interested in that stuff. She prefers face-to-face work.

Alex should have asked Puja for more details *before* she signed on to volunteer. Alex should have also considered the fact that, as smart and dedicated as she is, she's an unqualified teenager, and that social work is an adult career that requires specific schooling and certifications.

However, none of this means Alex should quit. She just needs to start from somewhere more practical. Social media is a good skill to learn in general, and even if she can't interface with the youth directly, she will definitely gain some knowledge and experience just by being in the office. Once she becomes closer to Puja, Alex can ask her questions about the field and get involved in different ways. In fact, Puja probably started in a similar position.

USE YOUR SCHOOL TO DEVELOP YOUR ACTIVISM

School is an easy channel for participating in activism. Your school may already have clubs focused on activism or inclusivity that you can join. You can also start your own club, which we discussed on page 101.

Much of activism is about raising awareness in your community. For instance, depending on your school's protocol, you can write a proposal to your administration to celebrate "climate week," in which all students learn about climate change and participate in meaningful, eco-friendly actions.

School also gives you access to a huge community of teachers, students, families, and coaches who might want to help. You can promote causes through your school newsletters or newspapers. You can attend school board meetings and speak up to the folks in charge. And you can encourage other people to do so as well—there is strength in numbers.

WHAT ABOUT ISSUES *IN* SCHOOL?

If you see an ongoing issue at your school, make change. School is one of your communities, and you and your classmates have a legal right to receive the best education possible in a safe, nondiscriminatory environment. Being both a Difficult Activist Bitch *and* a Difficult Scholarly Bitch, you know your rights.

Activism in school might mean calling out a classmate for making a racist comment. It might mean drafting a petition for a fairer dress code, then taking your petition to the principal and the school board. Or it could mean leading a student club called the Sexual Harassment Task Force, creating a safe place for students to discuss sexual harassment in school, support one another, and take action to promote a safe and healthy school environment. Activism within your school doesn't have to be a fight. You could tutor low-income kids for the SAT or get the school's permission to organize a litter cleanup in your school's neighborhood to get people thinking about trash in their community.

SHOULDA COULDA WOULDA

Have you ever wanted to change or speak up about something in your school, but you didn't?

Maybe you didn't feel empowered enough to fix the problem or it seemed like too much work or you worried that it could get someone in trouble. Consider what you *could* have done, though. Could you have spoken with a trusted teacher about the issue? Could you have created a petition and collected student signatures?

The answer depends on your specific issue. But if you explore these possibilities in detail, you'll be ready when you face the *next* issue in school.

A NOTE FROM MARY
CHANGE THE WORLD, YOUR WAY

On a hot and humid morning in Atlanta, I stood surrounded by people, white cane in one hand, a sign in the other. I was seventeen, traveling on my own for the first time, and standing at the starting line of my first ever civil rights march. Congressman John Lewis, a civil rights activist and Congressional representative, was saying some truly moving things through the microphone. Unfortunately, we could only catch every other word, since the sound quality was awful! For the record, this is a typical problem for large marches.

But it wasn't about hearing every word. It was about the unity and strength that I felt to my core. Most of the people in the march, which numbered about six hundred, were blind, and all of us believed that we have the right to equal opportunity.

I have been an activist for most of my life. For some of us who face discrimination on a daily basis, activism may not feel like a choice but a duty, because the alternative is the compromise of our dreams. However, activism is always a choice, and we don't have to do it alone! As a visibly disabled woman I have to be an advocate for myself on a constant basis. But I'm also passionate about opening the door for those who come after. Activism, even the kind that relates directly to your identity, does not need to be a heavy weight around your neck just because others expect it. Here are some tips on how to be a kick-ass activist on your own terms.

First, do not let others define who you are and what you care about. Maybe you are transgender, and so people expect you to devote yourself to trans-specific causes, but what you really want to be involved in is alleviating homelessness in your community. Go for it. It's your time and your passion that matter the most. Your unique perspective can only enrich any space you choose to occupy. On that note, do you feel you don't bring diversity to a cause? It's all the more reason to be involved and learn how you can be a strong ally. Marginalized and underrepresented minorities have no choice but to deal with the -isms of the world every day, so allies— people who choose to join our voices—not only serve to strengthen collective action, but they also affirm that we are seen and heard.

Second, figure out what role you want to play and what you want to get out of your experience. Whether you are stuffing envelopes or doing grassroots organizing, you are a leader in your own right. Embrace it and take the opportunity to learn. As an activist, I've been privileged to sit on nonprofit boards, speak at the United Nations, and meet amazing people I would never have met otherwise. Activism is a great way to build and strengthen community and connection.

Third, set boundaries. As I mentioned, the spaces I occupy, such as a top-ten business school or a corporate job, don't usually have a ton of people like me. So I become the go-to for literally everything everyone has ever wanted to know about blind people and disability. I make it clear, in a very friendly but firm way, that it is not my job to educate on a constant basis, and that I'm not just my disability or my gender or my race. I'm an interesting, multifaceted Difficult Bitch who really, really wants to talk about all the shoes she wants but can't afford! I've come to realize that being the best at what I do, in whatever space I'm in, is perhaps the most powerful way of being an activist. Being your truest self means that you are not only dismantling biases but also serving as a role model and trailblazer for those who will come after you.

Fourth, no matter what you do, always strive to be more inclusive. It is ironic that as we try to make the world a better place, we sometimes inadvertently exclude other marginalized voices from the conversation. It doesn't matter what your role in activism is; always think about how you can be more inclusive. Does everyone in your group look exactly the same or come from the same background? Ask yourself why that is and how you can change it. Is there a way to make your activist actions more accessible to people with disabilities? Are there ways that others from outside your group who care about the same cause can contribute? The power of activism comes from collective action. Being inclusive is not only the right thing but also the smart thing. If you can get a wide sample of the population to stand up for a cause you care about, you are more likely to create change.

At the end of the day, activism is one more piece that makes up the entire puzzle of who you are. There will be times in your life when all you can do is donate five dollars a month to a cause, and times when you step up to lead. Regardless, your activism and the energy you bring to it will make a difference in someone's life.

LOOK IN OTHER PLACES

If your school doesn't have what you need or if you're homeschooled, here are some other places to look for activist opportunities:

- Animal rescues are on the front lines of animal rights activism, but they also need day-to-day help.
- Community gardens are made by volunteers. You can help beautify your neighborhood or grow vegetables for underprivileged communities while learning about plants in the process.
- Hospitals often have volunteer programs in understaffed areas.
- Homes for the elderly often welcome volunteers to read aloud, play games, or just talk with residents.
- Food pantries or homeless shelters need help making, storing, and distributing food.
- Your community may have a youth mentoring program you can join, or you can offer free tutoring or lessons on your own.
- Churches and religious institutions often engage in activism, or they lend their spaces out to local activist groups for meetings.
- Nonprofit organizations are doing a lot of hard work to make change, and they usually need funds. You can hold an event, sell crafts or snacks, or get your school's permission to put a donation jar in the school cafeteria. All proceeds can go to an organization you care about.
- You can start your own movement with a hashtag, a story, some content, and a vision. This is a lofty goal, so maybe do some preliminary Difficult Bitch Activism before you aim for this one.

PEOPLE CAN BE IGNORANT AND CRUEL

When Emma González spoke out to Congress against gun violence in 2018, my jaw dropped in admiration. This poised, passionate student was standing up to the adults who had done nothing to protect her. How could Congress *not* listen to her? How could they *not* feel ashamed?

As usual, however, some politicians displayed their ignorance, and plenty of internet trolls spewed hatefulness. People made fun of her shaved head. They threw racist epithets at her. They made fun of her for being bisexual. They accused her of being paid by rival politicians. These people didn't represent everyone—she had many, many supporters. But their voices were still reaching Emma, who tweeted: "They hate us for smiling, they hate us for crying, they hate us for speaking, they hate us for being alive—they hate us. What's important to remember is that their argument against us is so weak and futile that they have to resort to attacking people delivering the message."

That's the ultimate Difficult Bitch tweet. Emma spoke her mind and didn't stoop to the trolls' level—in fact, she used their insults to strengthen her position. It's quite masterful.

A Difficult Activist Bitch knows that internet trolls do everything they can to be hurtful, and some are even dangerous. If you're leading a cause or putting yourself out there, please protect yourself. Don't engage with any trolls. Don't give out personal information. Even better, don't read the comments. Lean on your support system. If you read something hurtful, don't let it derail your important work.

Additionally, not everyone has to be a hardcore activist. Take breaks when you need to recharge. You can focus on smaller acts, like caring for friends and family. And don't neglect self-care. Improving your own well-being will uplift the people around you and will help you be more effective as an activist in the long run.

And if none of this motivates you to be an activist, remember: it will look great on your college application too.

BE YOUR OWN ROLE MODEL

You, as a Difficult Bitch, are a role model.

Kids are looking up to you. They're looking at how you tie your shoes, how you talk to adults, and how you rely on *yourself* rather than on others.

Once you recognize that your life today has a major impact on the future, you are officially a Difficult Future Bitch.

As Difficult Bitches, we *must* stand together and encourage future Difficult Bitches to stand up and be Difficult AF.

With that, the wonderful authors from this book are here to chime in about their inspirations.

AN INTERVIEW WITH SHARON

Who is your role model?
My role model is Octavia Butler, an award-winning science fiction author.

Why do you look up to her?
She broke down barriers and made space for herself with her writing, and today, her books are loved and respected as classics of the science fiction genre. She showed me that nerdy Black girls could make space for themselves in science fiction writing by working hard and believing in the importance of their voices. Whenever I read Butler's work, I am reminded that whatever story is in your heart to write, you must be true to it and share it with the world.

What makes you a Difficult Future Bitch?
I'm a Difficult Future Bitch because I love supporting women. It's how I think the world will be changed—by lifting each other up in big moments and small, in boardrooms and, heck, in public bathrooms too (shout-out to random heart-to-hearts with other women in nightclub restrooms).

When I write about vulnerable topics from a first-person perspective, I am honest, no matter how painful, because there is power in truth, and I want any other woman who may relate to know that she is not alone in the world. It's important to be brave when you write.

I am a mother, and every day I'm trying to be an example of what it looks like to never give up on yourself.

How can you become an even bigger and better Difficult Future Bitch?
I can stop doubting myself and stop apologizing for basically existing. I can own my worth and my beauty and my talent. I can stop thinking so much about things that don't matter,

like acne scars and what strangers think of me. I can educate myself more (like, what is going on with climate change? Asking for a friend).

Most importantly? I can stop being afraid to use my voice and write more.

AN INTERVIEW WITH ZARA

Who is your role model?

I have many role models, and one of them is Sophia Bush. You may know her as an actress on shows like *One Tree Hill* and *Chicago P.D.*, but she's also an incredible activist. She uses her platform of fame to spread awareness about what's going on in our world. She fights on behalf of marginalized groups. She's a supertalented, megasuccessful woman who doesn't just talk the talk where empowerment and equality are concerned. She actually walks the walk, and she does so while the world watches. It's incredibly inspiring.

Why do you look up to her?

Sophia shows us, time and time again, that she is more than one thing. She's a successful, driven woman who is so compassionate and brave. She proves you can love things like fashion and still be a woman of great substance. One time, I had a total fangirl moment and commented on her Instagram post. I wrote, "You have a beautiful soul, Sophia Bush." I think that about sums up why she's one of my role models.

What makes you a Difficult Future Bitch?

I'm a Difficult Future Bitch because I am a smart, funny, compassionate woman. I've learned how to empathize. I've chosen a life that makes me happy. I'm raising two wonderful, amazing humans. I've made a career doing something I love, even when it's hard. I enjoy my own company. I like who I am, and I like who I'm becoming.

How can you become an even bigger and better Difficult Future Bitch?

Where do I begin? I can work on all aspects of myself: my world view, my work ethic, my patience. I can learn more about politics and finances. I can do more for the environment. I can do more to teach my children that not everyone is as lucky as they are. I can admit I have more work to do.

AN INTERVIEW WITH HALLEY

Who is your role model?

My role model is a young woman named Haben Girma. She is the first deaf-blind woman to graduate from Harvard Law School. She is an author whose parents hail from Eritrea and Ethiopia. She also happens to be a good friend of mine.

Why do you look up to her?

Haben is one of the bravest people I know. She tirelessly travels the world championing disability rights and access. If someone tells her that she cannot do something—from surfing to improv comedy—she becomes even more motivated to make it work. She calls people out on ableist language. She becomes fast friends with people who have never spoken to a disabled person before, and she educates them about accessibility over and over again—no matter how frustrating that gets. She is pure grace. Also, she's hysterically funny.

I am not disabled. However, Haben is a hero to anyone who has to fight for rights.

What makes you a Difficult Future Bitch?

I've been through a lot as a woman, but I also recognize that I've been given a lot of privilege in this life, and I hope to use it for good. I want to keep learning, and I want everyone to have a seat at the table.

I also write. A lot. My work tackles everything from feminism to transgender health rights to information about sexual assault.

How can you become an even bigger and better Difficult Future Bitch?

I'm raising my daughter, Robin, to be a champion for social justice.

AN INTERVIEW WITH MARY

Who is your role model?

I am so fortunate to know so many Difficult Bitches who inspire and push me to be better every day. However, my forever role model is my mother, Clara. When I think about the person I am yet to become, she is the graceful, courageous, and authentic person that comes to mind.

Why do you look up to her?

At the age of twenty-six, my mother decided that she wanted a better life for my brother and me. So, she did everything she had to, packed a bag and came to the US. While she was here, she received the news that I was going blind. Instead of changing her mind and going back, she wisely decided that this was more of a reason for her to work to bring us here because it would be the only place I'd have an opportunity to have a successful life. Without my mom's strength and sacrifices, I would not be where I am today.

Through all her hardships, my mom maintains the most generous heart, an incredible sense of humor, and a willingness to reach out and help anyone who needs her help. She is one of the most honest people I know, and no matter where she goes and what she does, she does it with style. My mother was a hairdresser by profession, but after a few health issues came up and she could no longer work at a salon, she did housekeeping for hospitals and nursing homes. Every time she entered a patient's room, she brought in the energy of one who cares for all. She made them laugh and just open up to her. She knew those who felt lonely and made the effort to make sure they knew she saw them. At the end of the day, my mother's ability to have everyone she meets feel seen, heard, and supported is what makes her a superhero in my mind. She never doubted that I could do whatever I set my mind to, way before I believed it myself.

What makes you a Difficult Future Bitch?

I think that my curiosity and fierceness when it comes to advocating for the rights of others are some of my greater strengths. When it comes to standing up for what's right, I seldom think about what it means to speak truth to power, the fact of the matter is that if I can amplify the voices of those who have gone unheard, I will do whatever it takes. I also know that I don't know everything, and most of all—and this is an unbelievable fact even to me—there are times when I'm wrong! Seriously though, I always maintain a mindset of curiosity to learn from others, to understand where they are coming from. We know that changing hearts means that we listen, and we meet people where they are. Hence, my goal in life is to change hearts to make the world a fairer and more equitable place to different perspectives, speaking up when called for, and stepping back and amplifying the voices of others.

How can you become an even bigger and better Difficult Future Bitch?

I think most of us are familiar with impostor syndrome. It is when we feel that we aren't good enough, and that actually one of these days people will find out that we were not all that great all along. After finishing business school, I have been battling with impostor syndrome more than ever. Part of it is that during much of my business school career, I didn't have equal access to my educational materials in an accessible format, which left me feeling like I had to justify my value every single day. Add that to being the only one who brought the identities of visibly disabled, woman, and person of color into all the spaces I occupied, and it sometimes made me feel like I just had to take up less space.

Figuring out how to deal with impostor syndrome and maintaining that throughout my life will be a big step in my personal journey of growth. I've made some big gains, but there is still a long path ahead. I also know that I will forever be a work in progress—continuing to challenge my own world views and working to understand the experiences of others who are different from me is crucial. I also must not allow my self-doubt and fear of failure to hold me back from pursuing my dreams and ambitions. Last, and most important, finding ways to uplift and support all the Difficult Bitches coming up in the world after me, and trying my best to leave the spaces I occupy a tiny bit better than they were when I first walked in.

FURTHER READING

Books

Banks, Ailie. *The Book of Bitch*. Sydney: Allen & Unwin, 2020.
The Book of Bitch is an *A* to *Z* tribute to those standing up to societal expectations. Filled with quirky illustrations, this book celebrates the many facets of being a bitch.

Curtis, Scarlett. *Feminists Don't Wear Pink and Other Lies: Amazing Women on What the F-word Means to Them*. New York: Ballantine Books, 2018.
This collection of essays examines multiple women's personal journeys to embrace feminism and stand up for themselves.

Hanks, Julie Azevedo. *The Assertiveness Guide for Women: How to Communicate Your Needs, Set Healthy Boundaries & Transform Your Relationships*. Oakland: New Harbinger, 2016.
This guide teaches mindfulness, cognitive behavior therapy, and dialectical behavior therapy strategies to overcome barriers to assertiveness.

Rose, Amber. *How to Be a Bad Bitch*. New York: Gallery Books, 2015.
Model, entrepreneur, and pop culture personality Amber Rose describes how she emphasizes self-acceptance, confidence, and authenticity in all aspects of her life.

Sincero, Jen. *You Are a Badass: How to Stop Doubting Your Greatness and Start Living an Awesome Life*. Philadelphia: Running Press Adult, 2013.
This book contains stories, advice, and simple exercises to inspire readers to take control of their lives and start loving themselves for who they are.

Websites

Black Girls in Tech
https://www.blackgirlsintech.org/
Black Girls in Tech was created to be a safe community for Black women to support, encourage, and motivate one another throughout their journeys in the tech industry.

Black Girls Run
https://blackgirlsrun.com/
Black Girls Run is a fitness resource meant to encourage women to stay active and live a healthy lifestyle.

Girl Up
https://girlup.org/
Girl Up is an international organization that hosts leadership development programs to teach girls how to advocate for gender equality and social change.

Videos

"Cultivating Unconditional Self-Worth Adia Gooden TEDxDePaulUniversity." YouTube video, 15:20. Posted by TEDx Talks, May 30, 2018. https://www.youtube.com/watch?v=EirlZ7fy3bE. Psychologist Adia Gooden shares her journey to finding and accepting her own worth. She describes the difference between self-worth and self-esteem.

"The Likability Dilemma for Women Leaders Robin Hauser TEDxMarin." YouTube video, 10:42. Posted by TEDx Talks, November 8, 2019. https://www.youtube.com/watch?v=PYyBqs_x044. Speaker Robin Hauser describes the unconscious bias that causes people to believe that strong, assertive women are unlikable and how this bias impacts politics, education, and jobs.

"Why You Need to Be a Bitch Tabatha Coffey TEDxStLouisWomen." YouTube video, 11:59. Posted by TEDx Talks, November 22, 2017. https://www.youtube.com/watch?v=OUmFdTHTD8M. This TEDx Talk examines how the term *bitch* can be used to hurt or empower people. Speaker Tabatha Coffey shares her definition for *bitch*.

INDEX